inspirations

PAINT EFFECTS

25 decorative projects for the home

inspirations

PAINT EFFECTS

25 decorative projects for the home

MAGGIE PHILO

PHOTOGRAPHY BY ADRIAN TAYLOR

LORENZ BOOKS

This edition first published in 1998 by Lorenz Books

Lorenz Books is an imprint of
Anness Publishing Limited
Hermes House
88–89 Blackfriars Road
London SE1 8HA

This edition distributed in Canada by Raincoast Books
8680 Cambie Street
Vancouver
British Columbia V6P 6M9

ISBN 1 85967 602 2

A CIP catalogue record for this book is available from the British Library

Publisher: Joanna Lorenz
Project editor: Clare Nicholson
Photographer: Adrian Taylor
Designer: Bobbie Colgate-Stone
Stylist: Judy Williams
Illustrator: Madeleine David

Printed in Hong Kong/China

3 5 7 9 10 8 6 4 2

CONTENTS

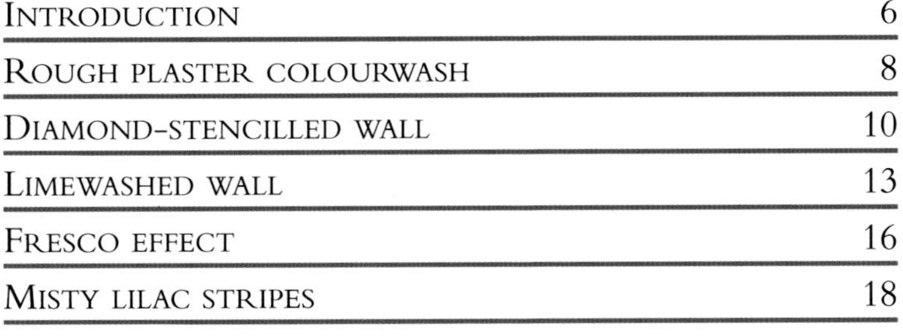

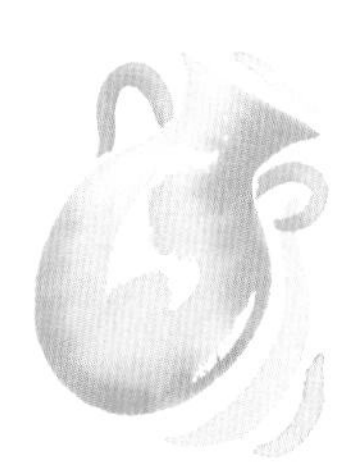

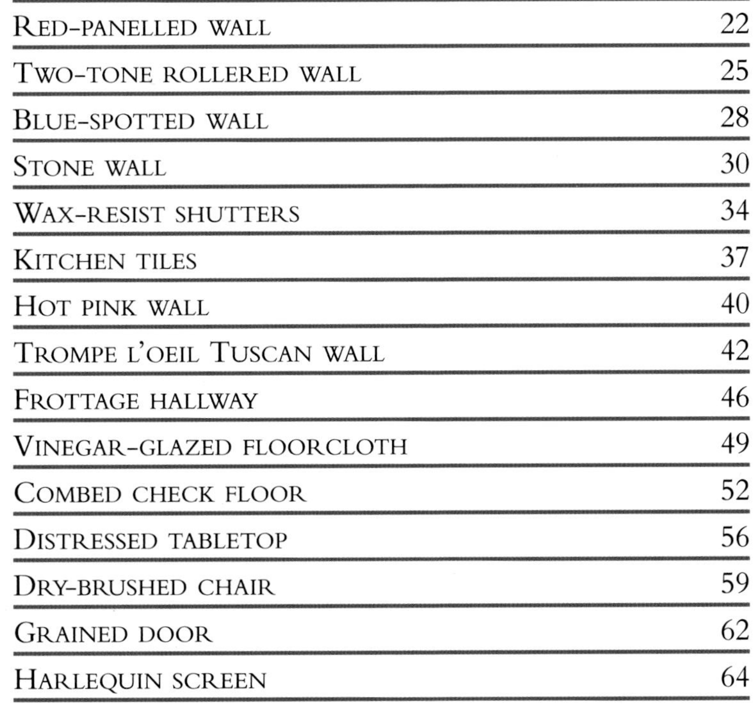

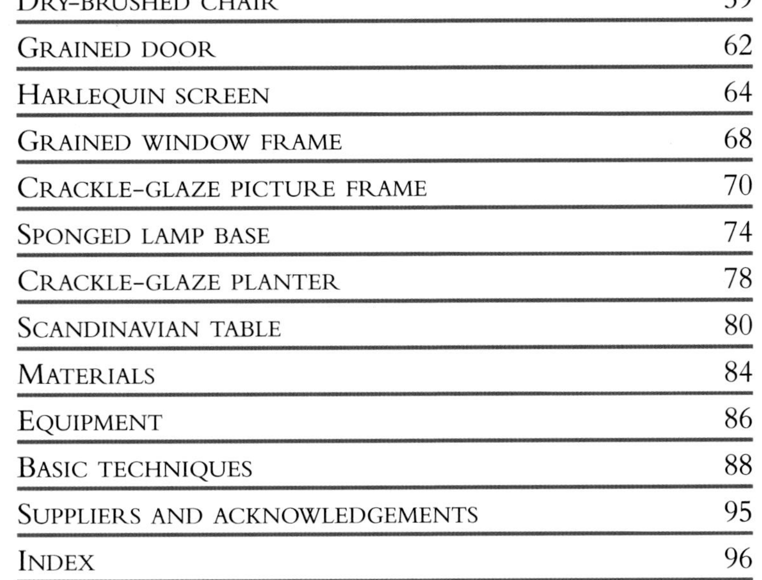

INTRODUCTION

I DO LOVE painting, but I hate sanding and I must admit that undercoating is a bit boring. Anything else I adore. There is real satisfaction in painting a surface - whether a wall, floor or piece of furniture - and getting immediate results. A room is transformed, even after just one coat of paint, but when you have added layer after layer to create the unique look you want, you will have your very own masterpiece.

The beauty of paint and paint effects is the incredible range of colours available to you. We can show only a limited number of colours in this book, but all the effects can be created in any colour. I admire homes that are colour co-ordinated from room to room, but when I am faced with a colour chart, I can't stop myself - I will want a blue, green and red. Do remember that if you have a particular colour in mind it can be specially mixed for you. To help you there is a section on mixing colours at the end of the book.

This comprehensive section also describes all the paint effects that form the basis of the stylish looks created in this book, plus the tools and materials you will need. None of the effects are difficult and with the full step-by-step instructions, you will find the most stunning looks easy to achieve, from creating a combed checked floor to a trompe l'oeil stone wall.

Deborah Barker

ROUGH PLASTER COLOURWASH

This sunny yellow wall was given a rough-textured look by trowelling on a ready-mixed medium (joint compound), available from DIY (hardware) stores, which is normally used for smoothing walls and ceilings that have unwanted texture. Colourwashing in two shades of yellow gives added depth and tone. The absorbent wall surface picks up varying degrees of paint, and there will be some areas which are not coloured at all, but this is all part of the attractive rural effect.

YOU WILL NEED

- medium (joint compound) for coating wall
- plasterer's trowel or large scraper
- large decorator's paintbrush
- white emulsion (latex) paint
- bright yellow emulsion (latex) paint, in two different shades
- household sponge

1 Apply the coating medium (joint compound) to the wall, using a plasterer's trowel or large scraper. You can choose to have a very rough effect or a smoother one. Leave to dry overnight.

2 Using a large decorator's paintbrush, paint the wall with two coats of white emulsion (latex), leaving each coat of paint to dry thoroughly.

3 Dilute one shade of yellow paint with about 75% water. Dip a damp sponge into the paint and wipe it over the wall, using plenty of arm movement as though you were cleaning it. Leave to dry.

4 Dilute the second shade of yellow paint with about 75% water and wipe it over the first colour in the same way.

DIAMOND-STENCILLED WALL

Here a stunning colour scheme is created by dragging a deep green glaze over a lime green base. The surface is then stencilled with shiny aluminium leaf diamonds, which stand out against the strong background. This paint finish would look very dramatic in a dining room, with muted lighting used just to catch the metallic diamond highlights.

YOU WILL NEED
- 2 large decorator's paintbrushes
- lime green emulsion (latex) paint
- monestial green and emerald green artist's acrylic paint
- acrylic scumble
- pencil
- stencil card (cardboard)
- craft knife
- cutting mat or thick card (cardboard)
- 2 artist's paintbrushes
- acrylic size
- aluminium leaf
- make-up brush
- clear shellac

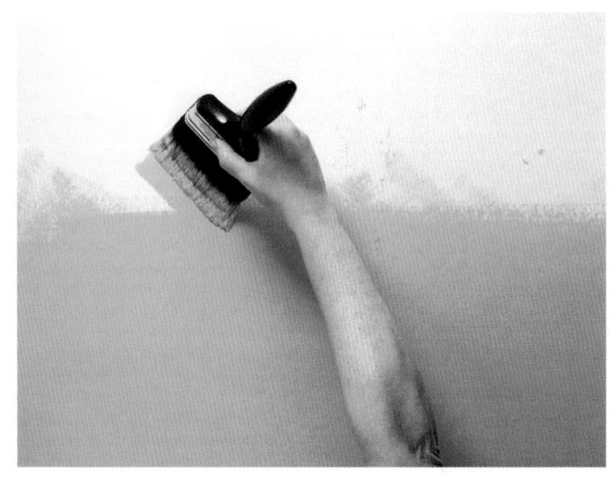

1 Using a large decorator's brush, paint the wall with lime green emulsion (latex). Leave to dry.

2 Mix a glaze from 1 part monestial green acrylic paint, 1 part emerald green acrylic paint and 6 parts acrylic scumble. Paint the glaze on to the wall with random brushstrokes.

3 Working quickly with a dry brush, go over the surface with long, downward strokes. Overlap the strokes and don't stop mid-stroke. Leave to dry.

4 Draw a small diamond shape in pencil on to stencil card (cardboard). Cut out, using a craft knife and cutting mat or thick card (cardboard).

5 Using an artist's paintbrush, apply a thin, even coat of acrylic size through the stencil card on to the wall. Repeat as many times as desired to make a decorative pattern.

6 After about 20 minutes, touch the size lightly with a finger to check that it has become tacky. Press a piece of aluminium leaf gently on to the size.

7 Working carefully, peel off the aluminium leaf, then brush off the excess with the make-up brush.

8 Using an artist's paintbrush, apply shellac over the diamond motifs. Leave to dry.

LIMEWASHED WALL

For an instant limewashed effect, apply white emulsion (latex) paint over a darker base with a dry brush, then remove some of the paint with a cloth soaked in methylated spirit (denatured alcohol). This is a good way to decorate uneven or damaged walls.

YOU WILL NEED
cream and white matt emulsion (flat latex) paint
2 large decorator's paintbrushes
old cloths
methylated spirit (denatured alcohol)
neutral wax

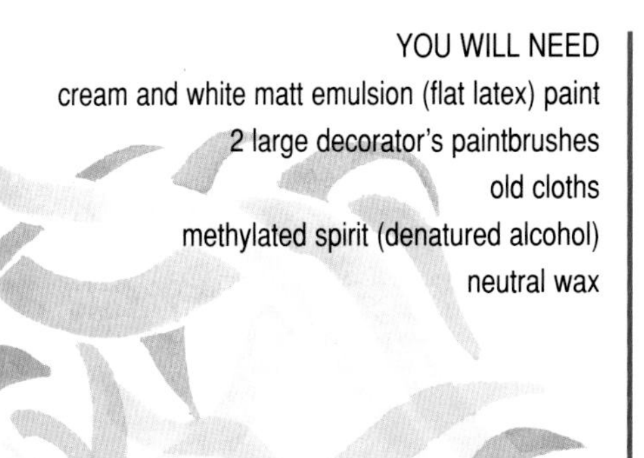

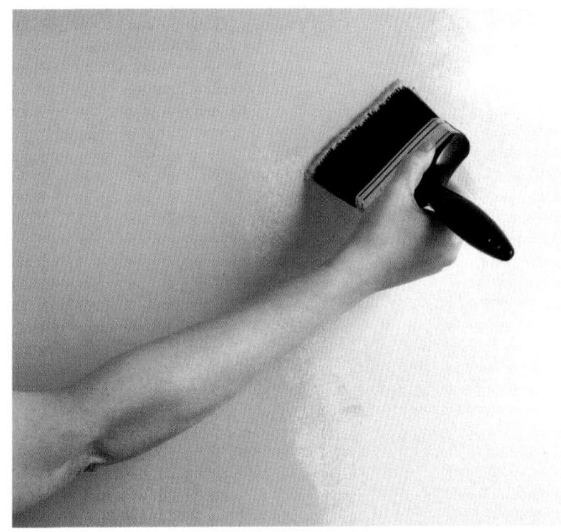

1 Paint the wall with a coat of cream emulsion (latex). Leave to dry.

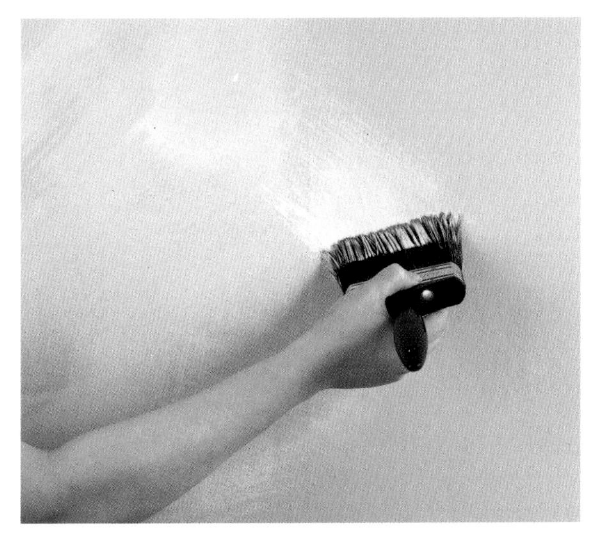

2 Dip the tip of the dry paintbrush into white emulsion (latex). Using random strokes, dry brush the paint on to the wall. Leave to dry.

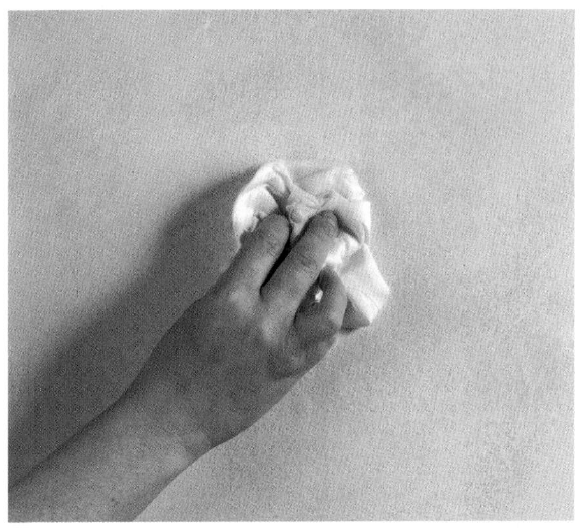

3 Using a cloth, rub methylated spirit (denatured alcohol) into the wall in some areas. Leave to dry.

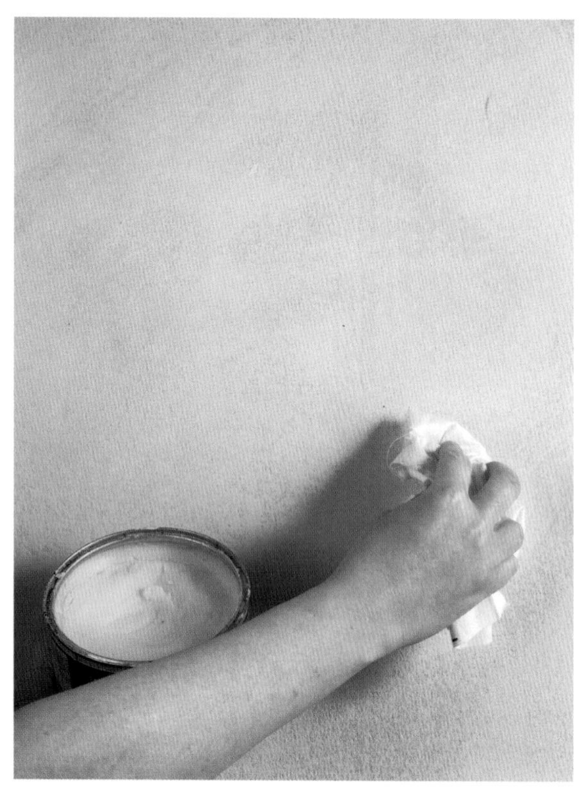

4 Using a clean cloth, rub wax into the wall to seal the paint.

FRESCO EFFECT

A dry brush and cloth are used here to soften rough brushstrokes and give the faded effect of Italian fresco painting. This wall treatment is the ideal background for a mural, so if you are feeling artistic you could paint a scene on top.

YOU WILL NEED
pale pink and ultramarine emulsion (latex) paint
acrylic scumble
2 large decorator's paintbrushes
old cloth

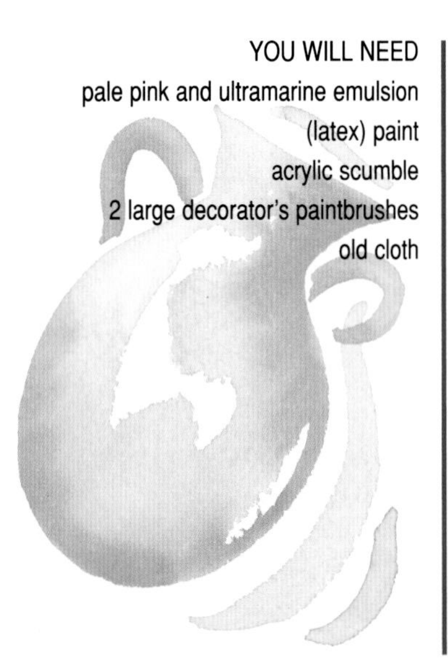

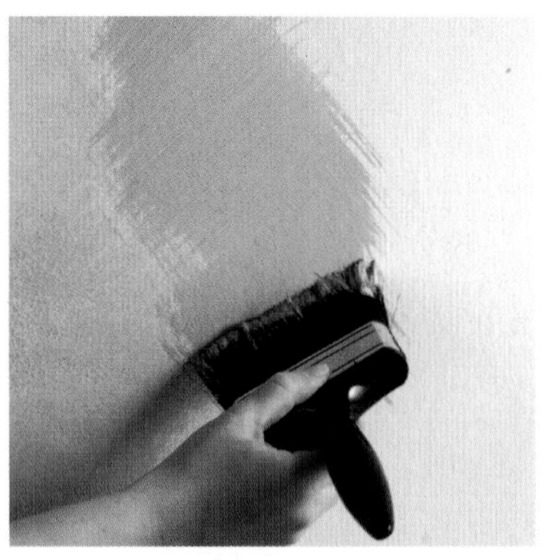

1 Mix a glaze of 1 part pale pink emulsion (latex) to 6 parts acrylic scumble. Paint the glaze on to the top half of the wall with random brushstrokes.

2 Using a dry brush, go over the top half of the wall to even out the brushstrokes.

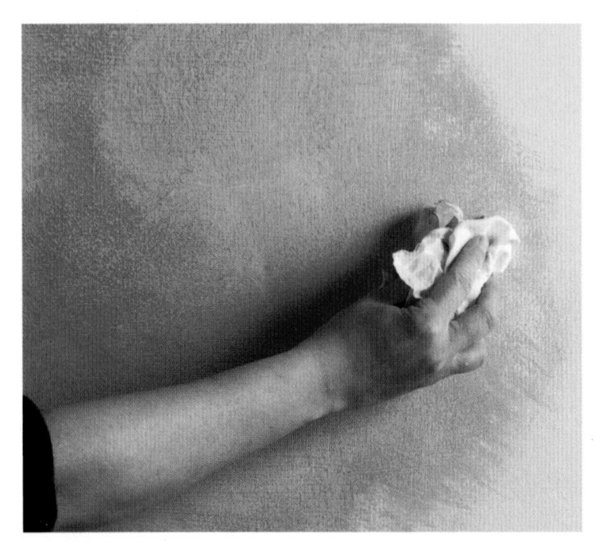

3 Rub a cloth into the glaze with circular motions, to produce the faded effect.

4 Repeat steps 1-3 on the bottom half of the wall, using ultramarine paint. Softly blend the two colours together with a dry brush.

STAFFORDSHIRE
CHARLOTTE

MISTY LILAC STRIPES

Here, wide stripes are painted and the wet paint dabbed with mutton cloth (stockinet) to soften the effect and blend in brushmarks. Careful measuring is required, but it is worth the effort. As an extra touch, paint a triangle at the top of each stripe. If you do not have a picture rail, take the stripes up to the top of the wall and place the triangles along the skirting board (baseboard).

YOU WILL NEED
- white silk finish emulsion (latex) paint
- paint roller and tray
- ruler and pencil
- plumbline
- masking tape
- lilac emulsion (latex) paint
- acrylic scumble
- medium decorator's paintbrush
- mutton cloth (stockinet)
- small piece of card (cardboard)
- scissors
- paint guard or strip of card (cardboard)

1 Paint the walls white, using a paint roller and tray. Mark the centre of the most important wall, below the picture rail (if you have one), with a pencil. Make marks 7.5 cm/3 in either side of this, then every 15 cm/6 in. Continue around the room until the marks meet at the least noticeable corner.

2 Hang a short length of plumbline from one of the marks, and mark with a dot where it rests. Hang the plumbline from this dot and mark where it rests. Continue down the wall. Repeat for each mark below the picture rail.

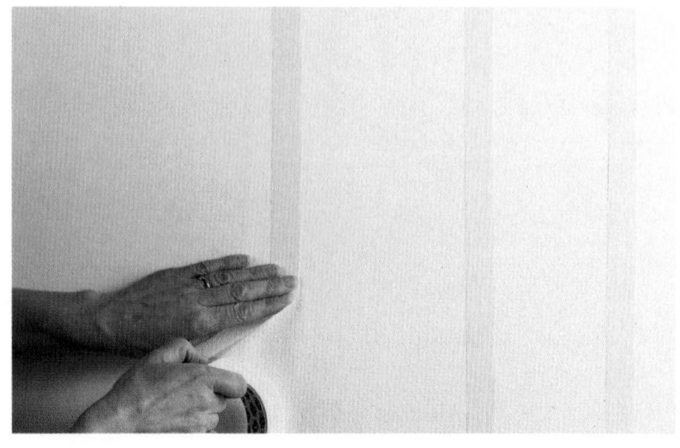

3 Starting in the centre of the wall, place strips of masking tape either side of the marked row of dots to give a 15 cm/6 in wide stripe. Repeat for the other rows of dots.

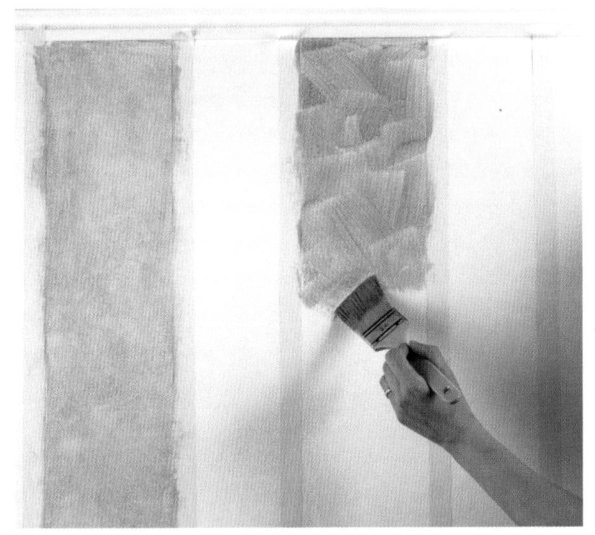

4 Dilute some of the lilac paint with about 25% water and 25% acrylic scumble. Brush on to a section of the first stripe. Complete each stripe in two or three stages, depending on the height of the room, blending the joins to get an even result.

5 Dab the wet paint lightly with a mutton cloth (stockinet) to smooth out the brushmarks. Complete all the stripes, then carefully peel away the masking tape and leave the paint to dry.

6 Cut a card (cardboard) triangle with a 15 cm/ 6 in base and measuring 10 cm/4 in from the base to the tip. Use this as a template to mark the centre of each of the stripes, lilac and white, 10 cm/ 4 in below the picture rail.

7 Working on one stripe at a time, place strips of masking tape between the top corners of the stripe and the marked dot, as shown.

8 Brush on the lilac paint mix, then dab the mutton cloth over the wet paint as before. Leave the paint to dry. Repeat for all the stripes.

9 Dilute some lilac paint with about 20 parts water. Brush over the wall in all directions to give a hint of colour to the white stripes.

10 Add a little paint to the remaining diluted mixture to strengthen the colour. Using a paint guard or strip of card (cardboard) to protect the painted wall, brush the paint on to the picture rail.

RED-PANELLED WALL

This bright red wall has been beautifully toned down with a translucent glaze of deep maroon acrylic paint mixed with scumble. The panel has been given a very simple trompe l'oeil treatment, using dark and light shades of paint to create a 3-D effect.

YOU WILL NEED
- bright red silk finish emulsion (satin finish latex) paint
- small and medium decorator's paintbrushes
- ruler and pencil
- spirit (carpenter's) level
- plumbline
- masking tape
- craft knife
- deep maroon, black and white artist's acrylic paint
- acrylic scumble
- mutton cloth (stockinet)
- clean cotton rag
- coarse-grade sandpaper

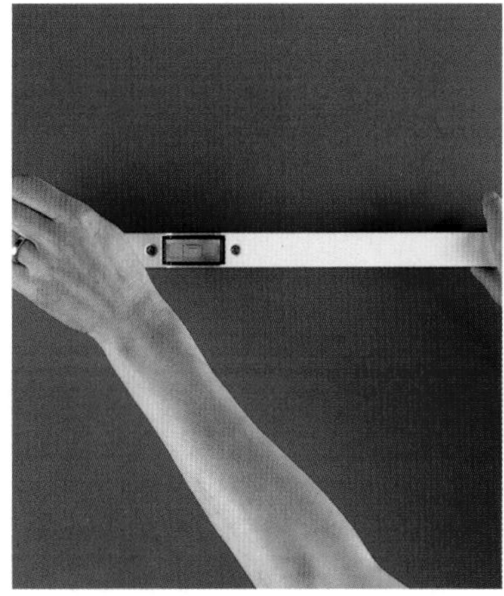

1 Paint the wall with two coats of red paint, leaving each to dry. Mark the centre top of the panel. Draw a horizontal line 30 cm/12 in either side of this mark.

2 Drop a line 90 cm/36 in down from each end of the drawn line and make a mark. Draw a line between all points to give a 60 x 90 cm/24 x 36 in panel.

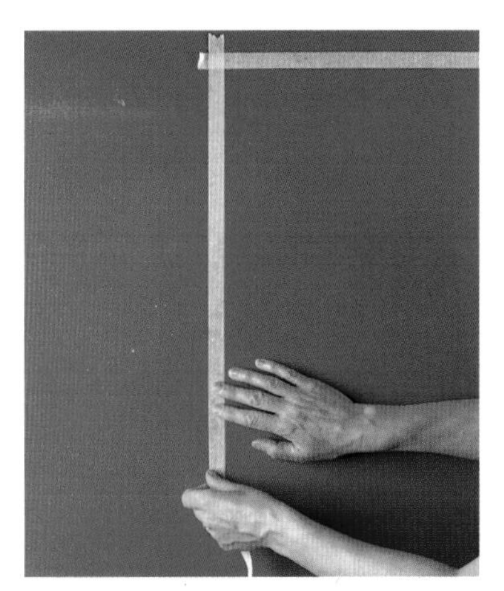

3 Place strips of masking tape around the panel. Neaten the corners with a craft knife.

4 Mix the maroon paint with acrylic scumble to the required colour. Brush this on to the panel.

5 Immediately dab a mutton cloth (stockinet) over the wet paint to even out the texture. ▶

6 Leave the paint to dry. Then, starting in a corner, brush the maroon glaze on to a section of the wall, roughly the same size as the panel. Dab it with the mutton cloth to blend the brushmarks as before, stopping just short of the edge of the panel. Roll up the cotton cloth into a sausage shape and then immediately roll it over the wet glaze, changing direction to give a more random effect. Leave to dry. Repeat with the rest of the wall.

7 Remove the masking tape. Place new strips of tape either side of the bright red line now revealed and trim. Mix a small amount of black acrylic paint with some of the maroon glaze. Brush this between the masking tape down one side of the panel, on the side where the light source is. Place a piece of coarse sandpaper diagonally at the top and clean off the glaze that extends beyond. Keeping the sandpaper in the same position, repeat on the top border of the panel.

8 Add a small amount of white acrylic paint to the maroon glaze and apply to the remaining two borders in the same way. Leave to dry, then carefully remove the masking tape.

TWO-TONE ROLLERED WALL

For this quick, ingenious paint effect, two shades of emulsion (latex) are placed next to each other in a paint tray and then rollered on to the wall together. Moving the roller in different directions blends the paint very effectively.

YOU WILL NEED
paint roller and tray
cream, yellow and terracotta emulsion (latex) paint

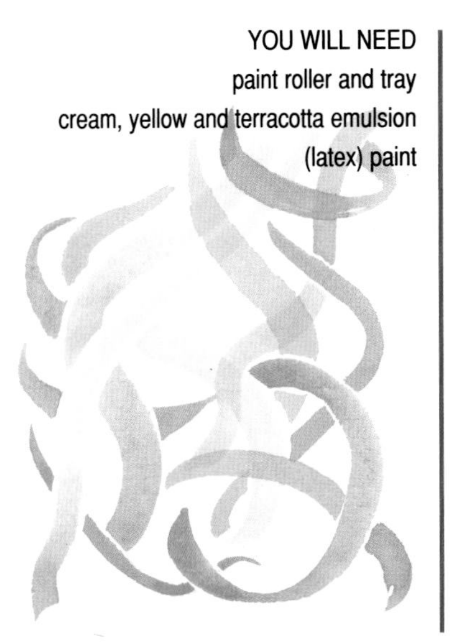

1 Paint the wall with a base coat of cream emulsion (latex), and leave to dry.

2 Pour the yellow and the terracotta emulsion (latex) into the paint tray together, half on each side. The two colours will sit side by side without mixing.

3 Paint the wall, applying the roller at a variety of different angles.

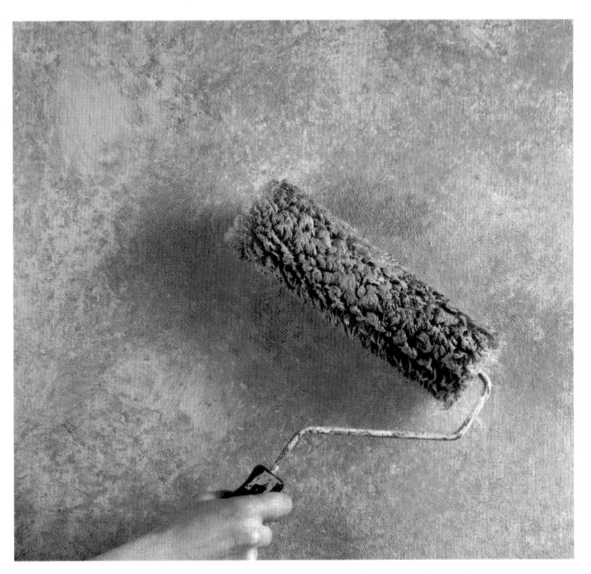

4 When complete, roller over the wall a few times to blend the paint, but don't overwork.

Above: Alternative colours – yellow and cream emulsion (latex) over a dark turquoise base coat.

Above: Complementary colours – light and mid-blue emulsion (latex) over a pale green base coat.

BLUE-SPOTTED WALL

The contrasting textures of natural and synthetic sponges are combined in this cheerful spotted wall, which is very quick and easy to do. A shadow effect is created by placing each blue spot slightly off-centre over a white one. This treatment would be ideal for a bathroom wall.

YOU WILL NEED
Prussian blue acrylic paint
acrylic scumble
old white plate
natural sponge
white and French navy matt emulsion (flat latex) paint
two sponge paint dabbers or small sponge paint roller

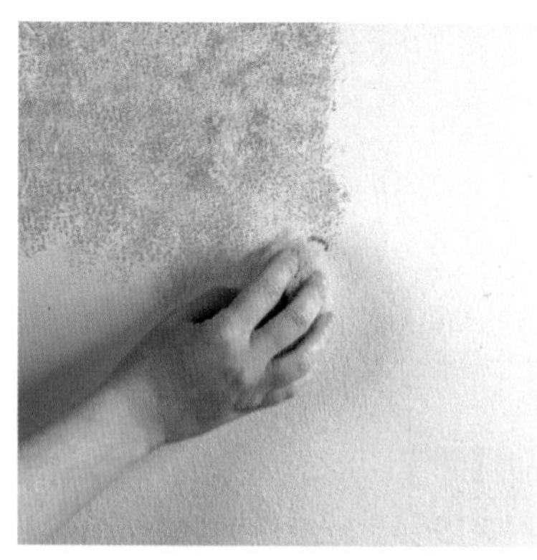

1 Mix a glaze of 1 part Prussian blue acrylic paint to 6 parts scumble. Dampen the sponge, then sponge the glaze on to the wall, rotating your wrist to vary the effect. Leave to dry.

2 Pour a little white emulsion (latex) on to a plate and spread into an even layer. Using a paint dabber or the end of a roller, stamp white spots randomly on to the wall. Leave to dry.

3 Using a clean paint dabber or the other end of the roller, repeat step 2 with French navy emulsion (latex) but stamp the blue spots on top of the white, leaving a small crescent of white. Leave to dry.

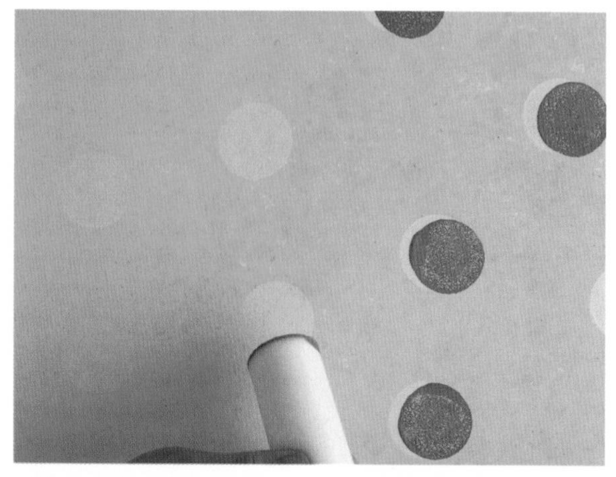

Above: This alternative colourway of red spots on a yellow sponged surface has been stamped with either end of a small paint roller.

STONE WALL

A subtle stone effect is created using several different techniques. Layers of paint are built up by stippling, sponging and rubbing colours on and off, and a hog softening brush is used to blend the wet glazes to look like stone. The wall is divided by a trompe l'oeil dado (chair) rail.

YOU WILL NEED

- large decorator's paintbrush
- cream emulsion (latex) paint
- spirit (carpenter's) level
- ruler
- pencil
- masking tape
- acrylic paint in raw umber, white and yellow ochre
- acrylic scumble
- decorator's block brush or stippling brush
- natural sponge
- hog softening brush
- old cloths
- fine artist's paintbrush

1 Using a large decorator's paintbrush, paint the wall with cream emulsion (latex). Leave to dry.

2 Using a level and ruler, draw pencil lines 6.5 cm/2½ in apart at dado (chair) rail height.

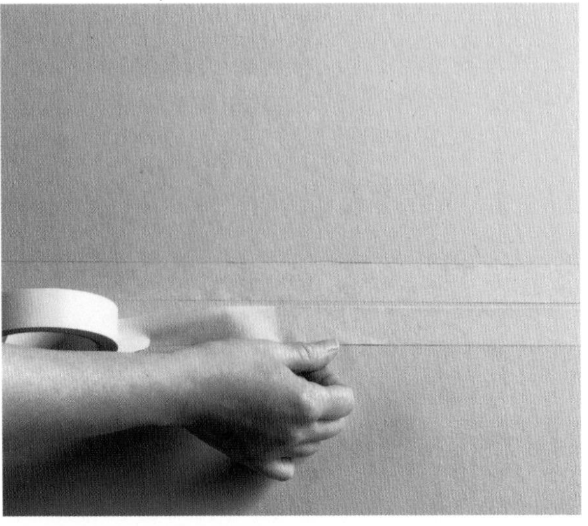

3 Place masking tape inside the two pencil lines, smoothing it in place with your fingers.

4 Mix a glaze of 1 part raw umber acrylic paint to 6 parts scumble. Stipple this on to the wall, using the tip of the block brush or stippling brush. Avoid the masked area. Leave to dry.

5 Mix a glaze with the white acrylic paint in the same way. Dampen a sponge and apply the glaze over the stippling, varying your hand position to avoid a uniform effect.

6 Using a hog softening brush, skim gently over the white glaze while it is still wet.

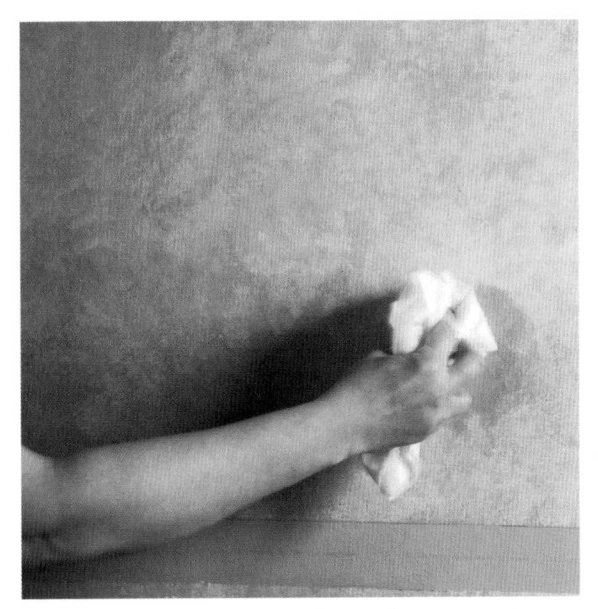

7 Mix a glaze with the yellow ochre paint as in step 4, but this time rub it into the wall with a cloth. Leave some areas of white glaze showing.

8 Using another dampened cloth, rub some areas to disperse the paint. Leave to dry.

9 Following an illustration or a piece of moulding, draw in the main lines of the false dado rail.

10 Highlight the lines in white acrylic paint, using a fine artist's paintbrush. Leave to dry.

11 Paint the darker areas in raw umber acrylic paint. Leave to dry. Mix in a little white acrylic paint and then add the softer, shadowed areas.

WAX-RESIST SHUTTERS

Give new wooden shutters or doors a weatherworn look by applying wax between two layers of different-coloured paint. Two colourways are shown – creamy yellow beneath bright blue, and pastel blue over candy pink for a sunny, Caribbean feel.

YOU WILL NEED
white acrylic primer
medium and small decorator's paintbrushes
soft yellow and bright blue or candy pink and pale blue matt emulsion (flat latex) paint
neutral wax
medium-grade sandpaper

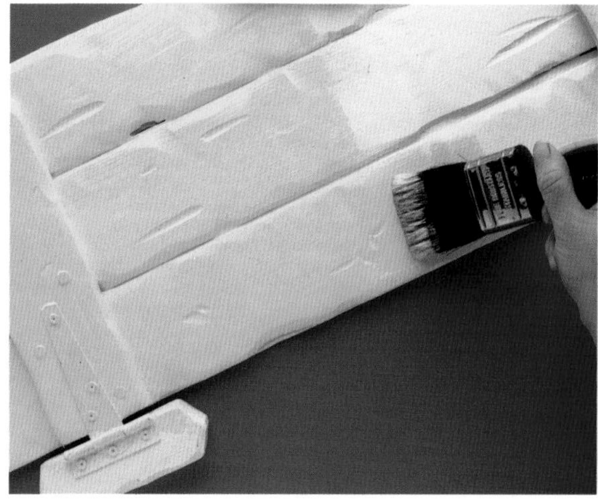

1 Paint the shutters with a coat of white primer and leave to dry. Paint with yellow emulsion (latex). Leave to dry.

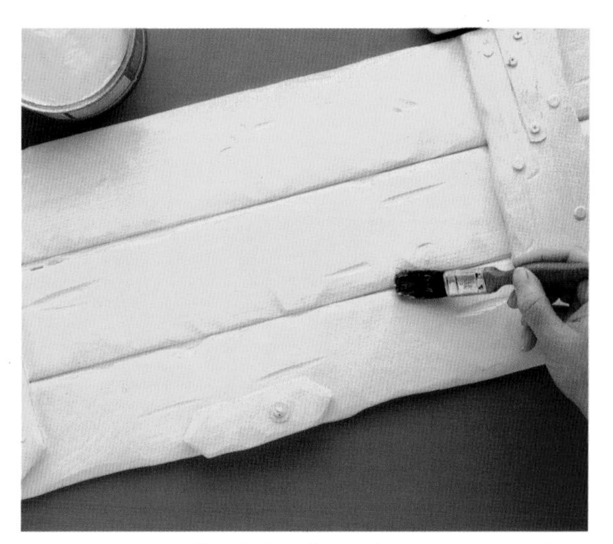

2 Using a small paintbrush, apply wax in areas that would receive wear and tear. Leave to dry.

3 Paint the shutters with blue emulsion (latex). Leave to dry.

4 Sand over the waxed areas to reveal the yellow base colour and create the "worn" effect.

Above: For an alternative colourway, paint candy pink emulsion (latex) over the primer.

Above: Apply wax as before, then paint with a pale blue top coat. Rub back with sandpaper to reveal areas of pink.

KITCHEN TILES

These clever "tiles" are, in fact, simple squares painted using three different techniques. Fine tape separates the tiles and is removed at the end to give the illusion of grouting. You can experiment with other paint effects (see Basic Techniques) and colours to create your own design, or leave some of the squares white as a contrast.

YOU WILL NEED
white silk finish emulsion (satin finish latex) paint
standard-size paint roller and tray
ruler and pencil
spirit (carpenter's) level
masking tape
fine line tape or car striping tape
wide easy-mask decorator's tape
ultramarine blue emulsion (latex) paint
small paint roller and tray
natural sponge
kitchen paper (paper towels)
4 cm/1½ in wide decorator's paintbrush
mutton cloth (stockinet)
craft knife (optional)

1 Paint the wall white, using a paint roller for an even texture. Decide on the width of your tiled panel. Mark the wall 45 cm/18 in above your work surface (counter) and in the centre of the width measurement.

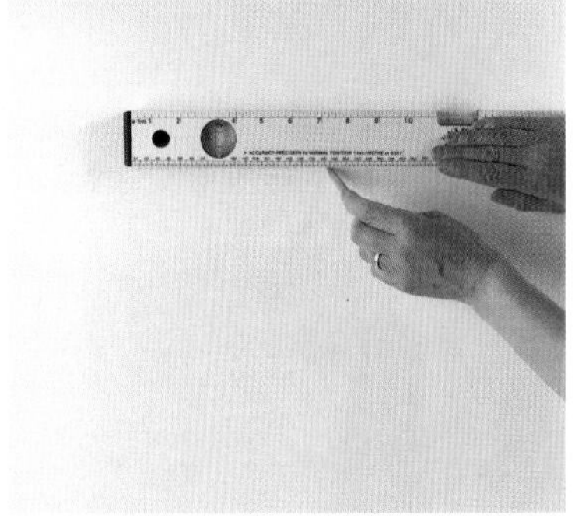

2 Draw a horizontal line at this height, using a spirit (carpenter's) level to make sure that it is straight. Place a strip of masking tape to sit above this line.

3 Mark dots along the tape at 15 cm/6 in intervals either side of the centre mark. Use the spirit level to draw vertical lines down the wall. Mark vertical dots at 15 cm/6 in intervals and draw horizontal lines.

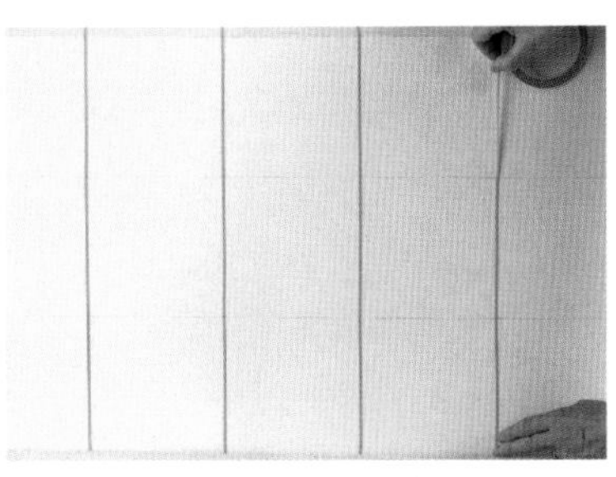

4 Place fine line or car striping tape over the lines in both directions. Smooth the tape into place with your fingers, pressing it down well to ensure that as little paint as possible will be able to seep underneath it.

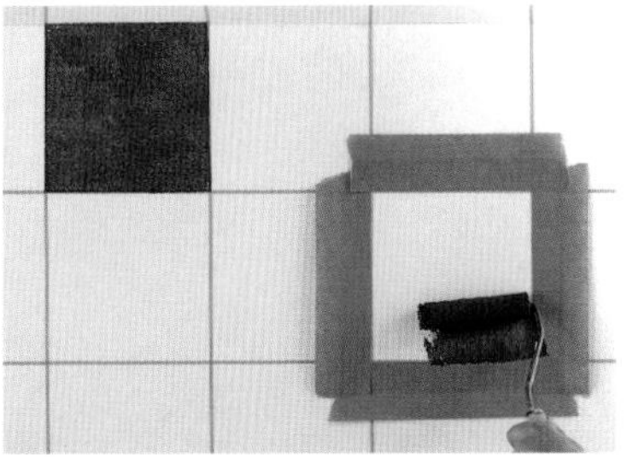

5 Place easy-mask tape around one square. Pour blue paint into the small tray and add 25% water. Apply an even coat of paint to the roller, then roll it over the square. Repeat for all the plain blue squares.

6 Mask off a square to be sponged. Dampen the sponge, dip it into the blue paint and dab the excess on to kitchen paper (paper towels). Sponge the paint on the square. Repeat for all the sponged squares.

7 Mask off a square to be dabbed with the mutton cloth (stockinet). Using a brush, apply the paint and then use the cloth to blend it. Continue as before.

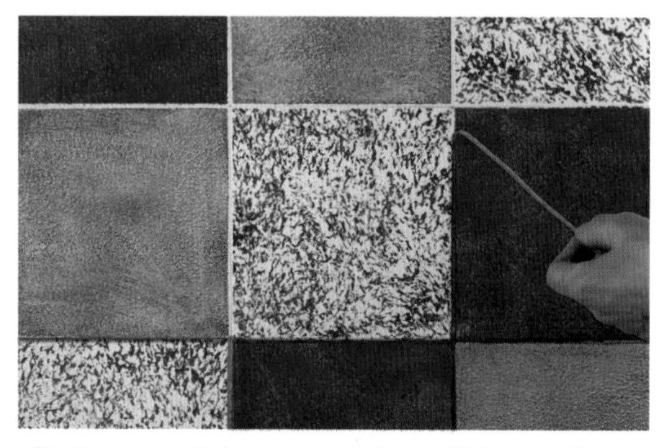

8 Remove all the tape and clean off the pencil marks. If paint has seeped under the tape in places, use a craft knife to scrape it off.

HOT PINK WALL

Here, pure powder pigment is mixed with neutral wax to achieve maximum colour intensity, quite unlike paint. The colour is worked in with vertical strokes to give a rough, dragged effect, whcih would look very striking in a contemporary setting.

YOU WILL NEED
magenta powder pigment
neutral wax
bowl
protective gloves
small decorator's paintbrush
old cloths

1 Mix 1 part magenta powder pigment to 2 parts wax in a bowl. Put on protective gloves.

2 Using a paintbrush, drag the mixture down the wall.

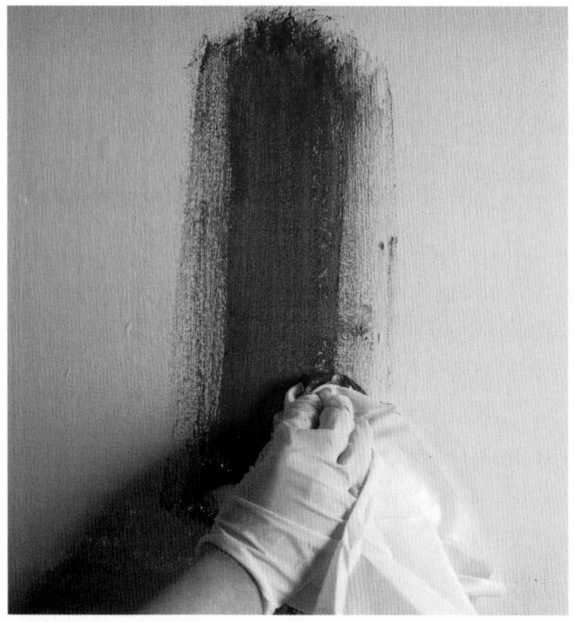

3 Using a cloth, rub the colour into the wall surface. Repeat over the rest of the wall.

Above: In this alternative colourway, violet powder pigment has been mixed with the wax.

TROMPE L'OEIL TUSCAN WALL

For a really dramatic effect, create an imitation Tuscan doorway on your wall. Paint on warm yellow, terracotta and green, and then sand back the paint to give the beautiful mellow appearance that normally only results from centuries of wear.

YOU WILL NEED
cream, warm yellow, terracotta and green emulsion (latex) paint
small, large and medium paintbrushes
scrap paper
paint roller and tray
pencil
set square (T square)
spirit (carpenter's) level and straightedge
string
masking tape
artist's paintbrush
hand sander
brown pencil

1 Experiment with mixing the colours. You can use quite strong shades as they will soften when they are sanded back.

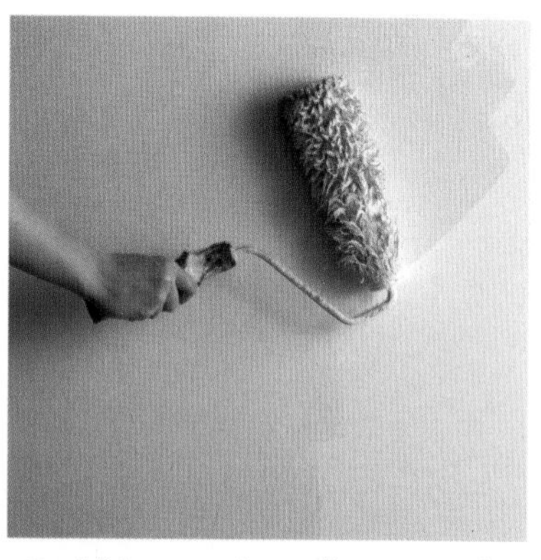

2 Using a paint roller, paint the wall surface with a base coat of cream emulsion (latex).

3 Wash over the base colour with warm yellow emulsion (latex), using a large paintbrush.

4 Draw your design to scale on paper, using a set square (T square).

5 Draw the straight lines of the doorway and border design on the wall, using a level and straightedge.

6 Draw the upper curve of the doorway, using a pencil tied to a piece of string as shown.

7 Mask off the areas of the design that will be painted terracotta with masking tape.

8 Paint these areas with the terracotta emulsion (latex), then remove the masking tape. Any smudging can be wiped off immediately.

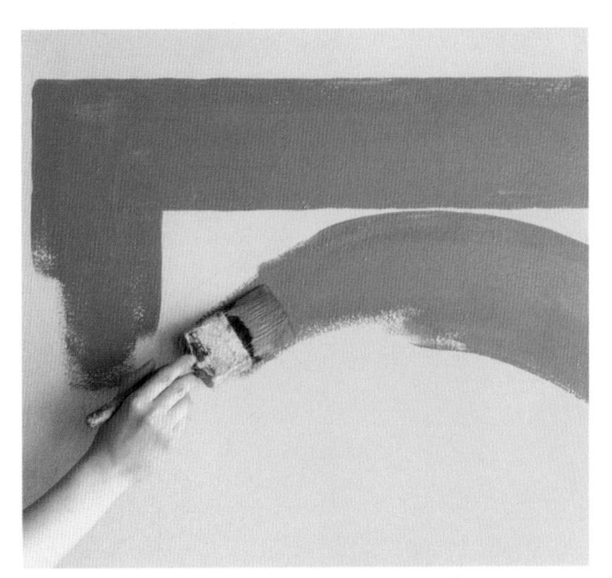

9 Using the medium paintbrush, paint the green area of the doorway. Use masking tape, if necessary, to mask off each area.

10 Using an artist's paintbrush, carefully paint a thin yellow outline around all the edges of the doorway. Leave to dry.

11 Lightly sand over the design, using a hand sander. Go back to the base coat in some areas and leave others untouched.

12 Wash over the design again with warm yellow emulsion (latex).

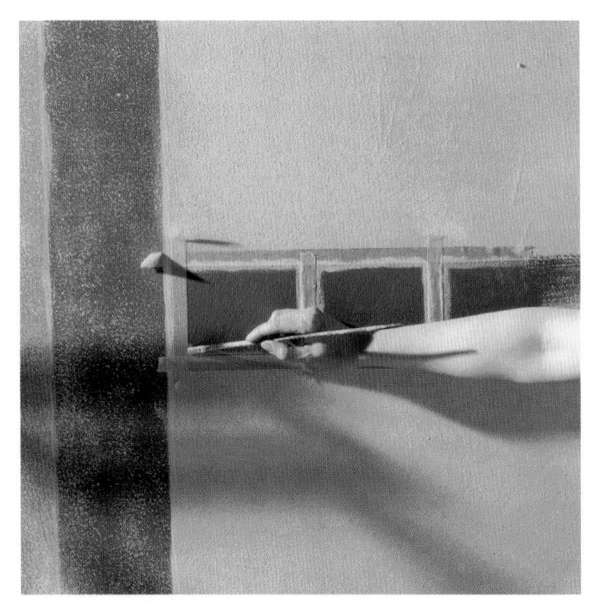

13 Mask off the squares in the border area with masking tape. Using an artist's paintbrush, outline each square in yellow and then immediately remove the masking tape.

14 Using a brown pencil, draw in fine lines in the semicircular "fanlight" ("transom") as shown.

FROTTAGE HALLWAY

The technique of texturing paint by pressing tissue paper over the wet surface is known as "frottage". Here, tone-on-tone in soft shades of green create the delicate effect shown at the top of the hallway. The pattern in the textured wallpaper below the dado (chair) rail has been highlighted by stippling on a darker green glaze, then wiping it off with a cloth to reveal the raised areas.

YOU WILL NEED

light, medium and dark shades of soft green and white silk finish emulsion (satin finish latex) paint (buy a dark shade and mix it with white to make the light and medium shades)
large and medium decorator's paintbrushes
medium shade of soft green matt emulsion (flat latex) paint
tissue paper
acrylic scumble
stippling brush
clean cotton rag

1 Paint the upper part of the wall with two coats of light green silk finish paint, leaving each to dry.

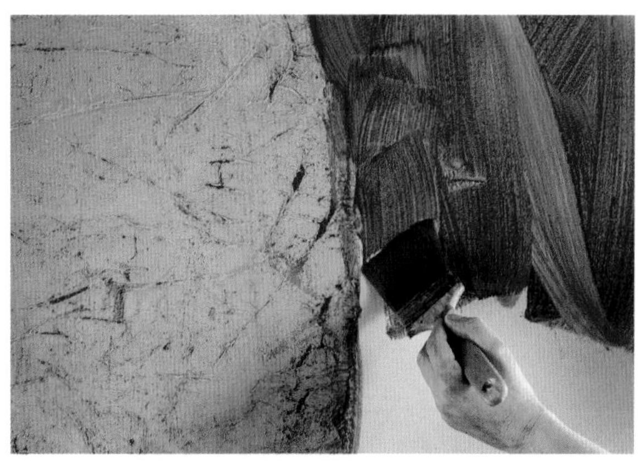

2 Dilute the matt (flat) green paint with about 20% water. Brush this on to a section of the wall.

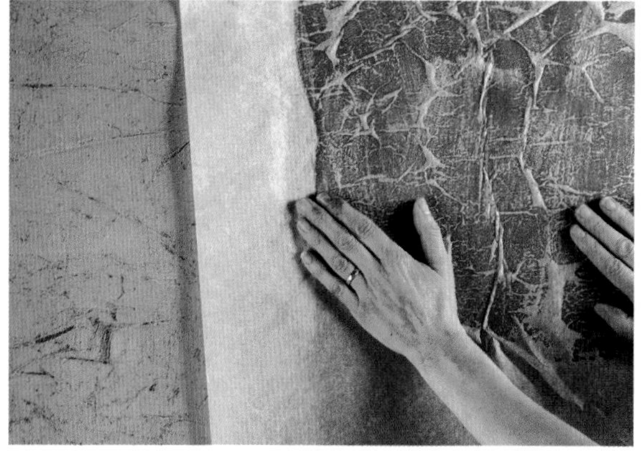

3 Immediately press a sheet of tissue paper over the entire surface except for a narrow band adjacent to the next section you will be working. Work on a manageable area at a time so that you can keep the edge wet. Better still, ask someone to assist you – one brushing, one following with the tissue paper. ▶

4 Carefully peel back the tissue paper to reveal most of the base colour.

5 Brush on two coats of medium green silk finish paint over the textured wallpaper below the dado (chair) rail, leaving each to dry. If the wallpaper is new, it may bubble, but it will shrink back when dry.

6 Mix dark green silk finish paint with acrylic scumble in a ratio of one part paint to six parts scumble. Brush this glaze on to a section of the wallpaper.

7 Immediately dab over the wet glaze with a stippling brush to eliminate brushmarks and even out the texture.

8 Wipe a cotton cloth gently over the stippled glaze to remove it from the raised areas of the wallpaper. Complete the wall section by section. Paint the dado rail with white paint, leave to dry and then brush over the dark green glaze.

VINEGAR-GLAZED FLOORCLOTH

Painted floorcloths were popular with the early American settlers as cheap, handmade alternatives to carpets. This one is painted with vinegar glaze and decorated with patterns, using a cork and other simple objects as stamps. Dark shellac gives an antique finish.

YOU WILL NEED

heavyweight cotton duck canvas (from artist's suppliers), 7.5 cm/3 in larger all round than the finished floorcloth
staple gun or hammer and tacks
white acrylic wood primer
large and medium decorator's paintbrushes
fine-grade sandpaper
set square (T square)
pencil
large scissors
PVA (white) glue and brush
2.5 cm/1 in masking tape
dessertspoon
bright red emulsion (latex) paint
gloss acrylic floor varnish and brush – use matt (flat) acrylic varnish if preferred
1 cm/½ in masking tape
malt vinegar
sugar
bowl and spoon
dark ultramarine powder pigment
reusable tacky adhesive
old cloth
cork
craft knife
dark shellac
floor varnish

PREPARATION

Stretch the canvas across an old door or tabletop and staple or tack in place. Paint with three or four coats of primer, leaving to dry between coats, then sand to give a smooth surface. Using a set square (T square), check that the canvas is square and trim if not. Mark a pencil border 2.5 cm/1 in from the edge. Cut diagonally across each corner, through the point where the pencil lines cross.

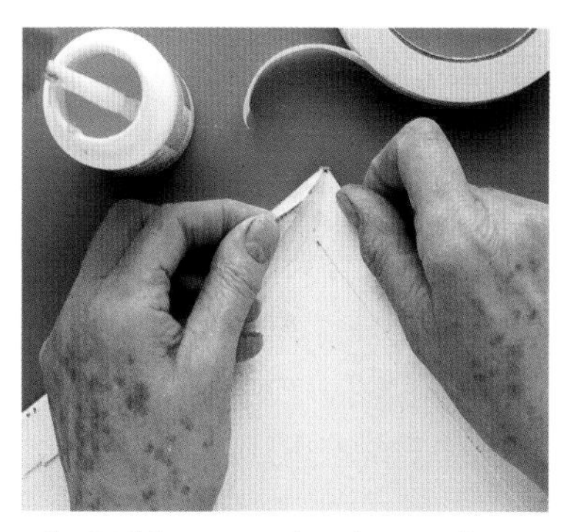

1 Fold over each edge to the pencil line. Glue and then secure with masking tape until dry. Rub the edges firmly with a dessertspoon. Sand the edges where the primer has cracked.

2 Turn the canvas to the right side. Using masking tape, mark a wide border. Paint with bright red emulsion (latex), carrying the paint over the outer edges. When dry, apply a coat of floor varnish. Leave to dry.

3 Remove the masking tape and tidy any ragged edges with extra paint. When dry, place 1 cm/½ in masking tape around the outer edge to a depth of 1 cm/½ in. Repeat around the inner edge of the border.

4 Mix 150 ml/¼ pint/⅝ cup malt vinegar with 1 teaspoon sugar. Add up to 2 tablespoons of dark ultramarine pigment and stir well – the glaze should flow on smoothly. Paint the glaze over the red border.

5 While the ultramarine glaze is still wet, make patterns by pressing the reusable tacky adhesive on top and then removing it.

6 Copy the patterns shown or experiment with your own. Wipe the glaze with a damp cloth if you make a mistake. The glaze will take about 15 minutes to dry.

7 Using a craft knife, cut a hole in one end of the cork. Paint the glaze over the centre panel. While still wet, stamp a pattern of circles and lines.

8 Cut a square at the other end of the cork to make a different stamp. Experiment with other objects. Use the reusable tacky adhesive to make additional lines and curves.

9 When dry, remove the masking tape. Tidy the edges with a damp cloth wound around your finger. Apply a coat of dark shellac, then several coats of floor varnish, allowing the canvas to dry between coats. Leave for at least 4 days before using.

COMBED CHECK FLOOR

A simple combing technique has been used to decorate this warm, sunny floor. You can experiment with other patterns instead of the traditional wave pattern shown here. Using a hardboard template to draw the squares saves the chore of measuring and marking out the floor before you start.

YOU WILL NEED

- yellow ochre, orange and red emulsion (latex) paint
- medium decorator's paintbrush
- 30 cm/12 in wide piece of hardboard
- pencil
- masking tape
- acrylic scumble
- rubber comb
- acrylic floor varnish and brush

1 Paint the floor with two coats of yellow ochre emulsion (latex), leaving each to dry.

2 Starting in the corner most on view, place the piece of hardboard against the side of the wall. Draw pencil lines widthways across the room. Return to the same corner and draw lines lengthways to form a grid.

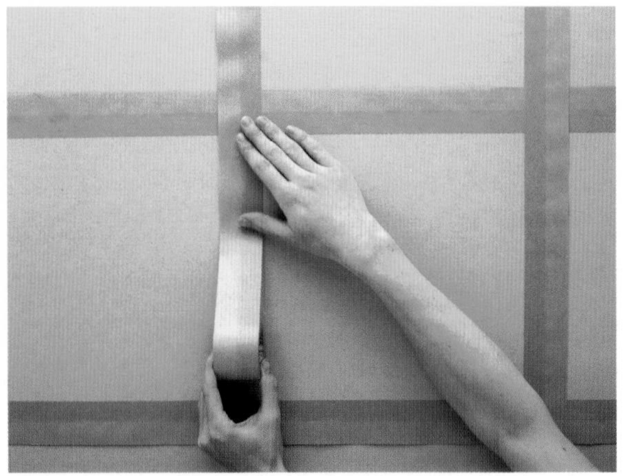

3 Place masking tape on the outside of alternate lines, both horizontally and vertically.

4 Mix some scumble into the orange emulsion (latex). Paint this mixture on to one square (you will need to work on one at a time so that the paint remains wet).

5 Run the comb through the paint, twisting your hand slightly to form a wave pattern. Repeat the process with the orange squares on alternate rows. Leave to dry, then remove the masking tape.

6 Place masking tape the other side of those squares previously marked. Paint these, one at a time, with red emulsion (latex) mixed with scumble.

7 Run the comb through the wet paint, this time in the opposite direction. Half the squares on the floor will now be painted.

8 To complete the remaining squares, simply mask each square individually and then paint in the appropriate colour.

9 Comb each of the squares as you go, while the paint is still wet.

10 When the paint is dry, seal the floor with three coats of acrylic floor varnish.

DISTRESSED TABLETOP

A junkshop buy can be transformed with a fashionably distressed look in shades of blue paint. Petroleum jelly and candle wax resist the paint in different ways. The petroleum jelly is applied to the tabletop in the main areas of natural wear and tear; the candle wax is then used along the edges of the tabletop, giving a more subtle effect.

YOU WILL NEED
- sanding block and medium-grade sandpaper
- navy blue, pale blue and mid-blue emulsion (latex) paint
- small decorator's paintbrush
- petroleum jelly and brush
- old cloth
- candle
- matt (flat) acrylic varnish and brush

1 Sand the tabletop to provide a key for the paint.

2 Paint with the navy blue emulsion (latex). Leave to dry.

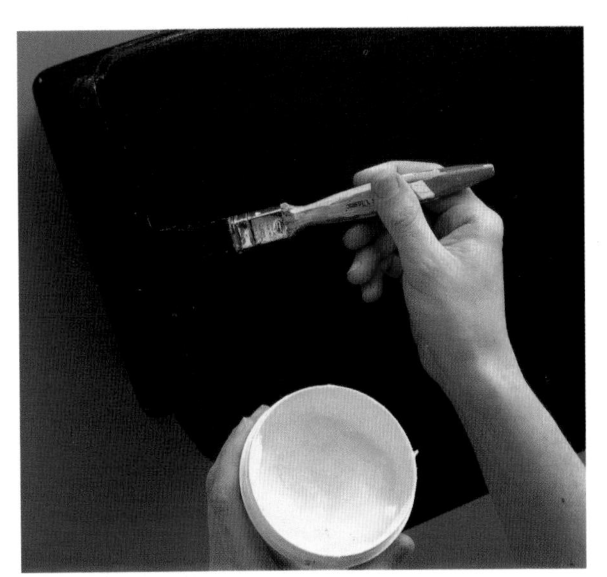

3 Brush on blobs of petroleum jelly, working inwards from the edges of the table.

4 Paint with pale blue emulsion (latex), applying the brushstrokes in the same direction – don't cover the surface completely. Leave to dry.

5 Wipe over with a cloth and soapy water. In the areas where the petroleum jelly has been applied, the pale blue paint will come away, revealing the navy blue base coat.

6 Rub over the surface of the table with candle wax, concentrating on the edges.

7 Paint the table with mid-blue emulsion (latex), again applying the brushstrokes in the same direction. Leave to dry.

8 Rub over the surface with sandpaper. Where the candle wax has been applied, the mid-blue paint will be removed. Seal with two coats of varnish.

DRY-BRUSHED CHAIR

A soft, distressed look is achieved by dry brushing off-white paint over a light brown base painted to imitate wood. This is another excellent technique for making a tired old piece of furniture look desirably aged.

YOU WILL NEED
old cloth
sanding block and medium-grade sandpaper
pale terracotta and off-white emulsion (latex) paint
small decorator's paintbrush
sponge
matt (flat) acrylic varnish and brush

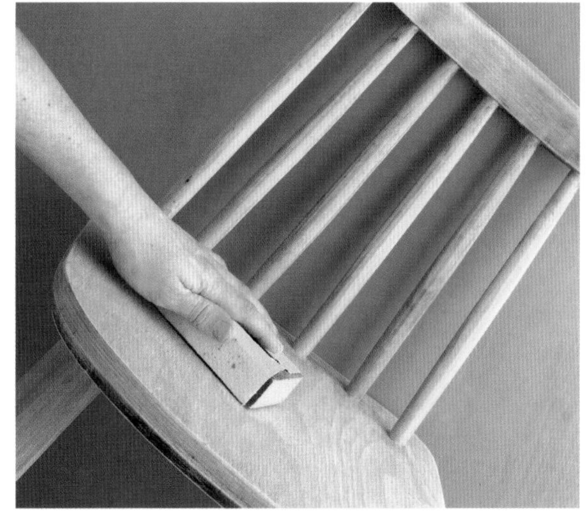

1 Wipe over the chair with a damp cloth, then sand it in the direction of the grain.

2 Mix the pale terracotta emulsion (latex) 50/50 with water. Paint the chair.

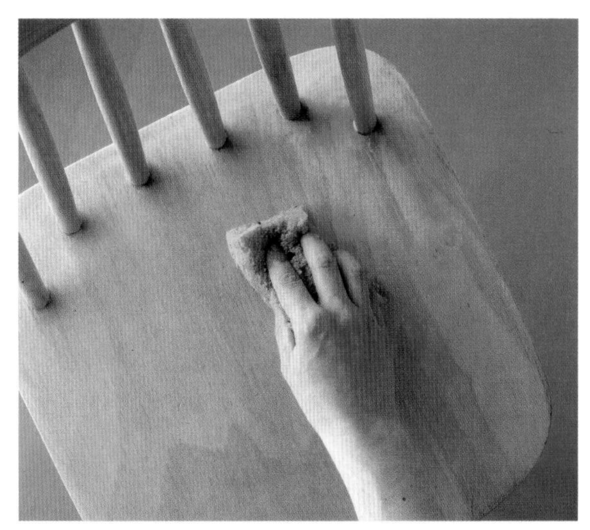

3 Using a sponge dampened with water, carefully remove the excess paint mixture.

4 Using a dry brush, apply the off-white emulsion (latex) over the chair. At the angles, flick the paint from the base upwards.

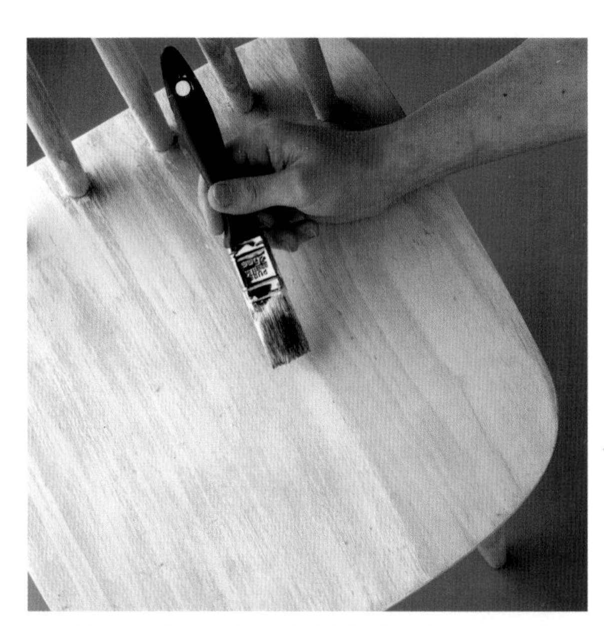

5 For the flat surfaces, hold the brush at an angle and apply the paint with minimal pressure. Seal with two coats of varnish.

GRAINED DOOR

This strongly textured combed graining is achieved by mixing wall filler with sky blue emulsion (latex). Lime green paint is then brushed over the blue and sanded off when dry to give a surprisingly subtle effect.

YOU WILL NEED
medium-grade sandpaper
sky blue and lime green emulsion (latex) paint
medium decorator's paintbrush
wall filler
rubber comb
matt (flat) acrylic varnish and brush

1 Sand the door and then paint it with a base coat of sky blue emulsion (latex). Leave to dry.

2 Mix 25% filler with 75% sky blue emulsion (latex). Paint on to the door, working on one small section at a time. While still wet, comb in lines, following the grain. Leave to dry.

3 Paint the door with a thin coat of lime green emulsion (latex), applying the paint in the same direction as the combing. Leave to dry.

4 Sand the door, revealing lines of blue paint beneath the lime green top coat. Seal with two coats of acrylic varnish.

HARLEQUIN SCREEN

Two simple paint techniques – stippling and rag rolling – are used here to great effect. Choose bright shades of paint as the colours will be softened by the white-tinted scumble glaze.

YOU WILL NEED
three-panel screen with curved top
screwdriver
cream emulsion (latex) paint
medium decorator's brush
fine-grade sandpaper
1 cm/½ in wide masking tape
1 cm/½ in wide flexible masking tape
long ruler or straight piece of wood
water-soluble marker pencil
fine line tape or car striping tape
wide easy-mask decorator's tape
stencil brush
kitchen paper (paper towels)
white palette or old white plate
emulsion (latex) paint in turquoise, red, yellow and green
matt (flat) varnish and brush
white acrylic paint
acrylic scumble
cotton cloth
gold acrylic paint
gold gouache paint
small stencil brush

PREPARATION

It is best to remove the hinges before sanding the surfaces to be decorated. Apply cream emulsion (latex) and leave to dry, then sand to give a smooth surface. Refer to the artworks at the back of the book for templates of how to mark up the screen.

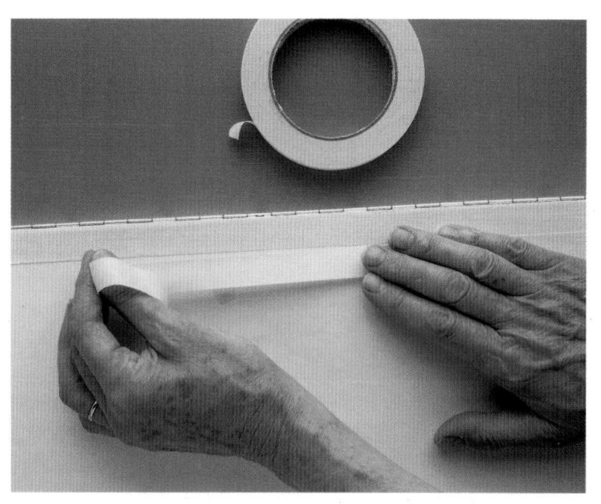

1 Place masking tape close to the edge of the screen along the outer borders of the two outer panels, and along the base of all three panels. Place a second line of tape next to the first.

2 Remove the outer tape, leaving a 1 cm/½ in border along the edge of the screen. Smooth down the remaining tape. Using flexible masking tape, repeat steps 1 and 2 along the top of all three panels.

3 Measure the height of the screen at the longest point and divide by six. Draw a vertical line halfway across the panel. Mark the centre point and two equally spaced points either side. Return to the centre point and divide the panel horizontally into four equal points, one each side of the central line. Draw a grid of equal-sized oblongs, four across and six down. Repeat for the other panels.

4 Lay fine line tape or car striping tape from the centre point at the top of each panel diagonally to the far right-hand corner of the next space. Continue from the far right-hand corner through the centre point until all the lines are marked with tape. Repeat in the opposite direction to make a diamond pattern. Secure the tape at the sides of the panel with a small piece of masking tape.

5 Using the wide easy-mask decorator's tape, mask off the diamonds that are to be painted in the first colour. Follow the picture of the finished screen for colour reference.

6 Bind 2.5 cm/1 in at the base of the stencil brush with masking tape. Dip the brush into the first colour, wipe the surplus on kitchen paper (paper towels) until the brush is fairly dry, then stipple the masked diamonds. Work out to the masking tape, using a firm pouncing motion. Leave to dry. Using the other colours, stipple all the diamonds.

7 When all the paint is dry, remove the fine line tape. Apply a coat of matt (flat) varnish and leave to dry. Mix a little white acrylic paint into the scumble to make a glaze. Paint this over the diamonds.

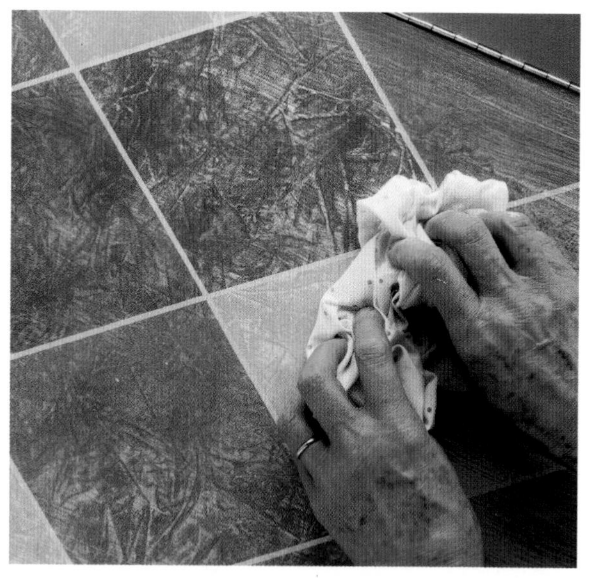

8 Holding a crumpled cloth between both hands, roll it down each panel while the glaze is still wet, moving your hands in different directions. Leave the glaze to dry.

9 Apply another coat of varnish. When this is dry, remove the masking tape from the borders of the diamonds.

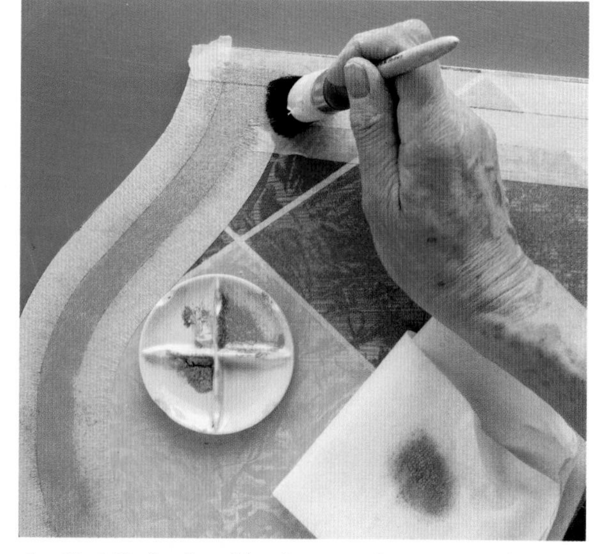

10 Mix both gold paints together. Lay masking tape either side of the cream borders. Stipple the gold paint on with a small stencil brush. Leave to dry, then remove the tape. Apply a final coat of varnish. When dry, replace the screen hinges.

GRAINED WINDOW FRAME

Here, extra interest is added to a window frame by decorating it with a subtle imitation wood pattern. The same treatment would work well on a wide picture frame. To hide a boring view, stencil the bottom panes of glass with frosted stars.

YOU WILL NEED
medium- and coarse-grade sandpaper
pale blue-green vinyl silk paint
medium decorator's paintbrush
deep blue-green matt emulsion (flat latex) paint
water-based scumble
heart grainer (rocker)
old cloth
gloss acrylic varnish and brush
rubber comb
star stencil
masking tape
stencil brush
acrylic frosting varnish

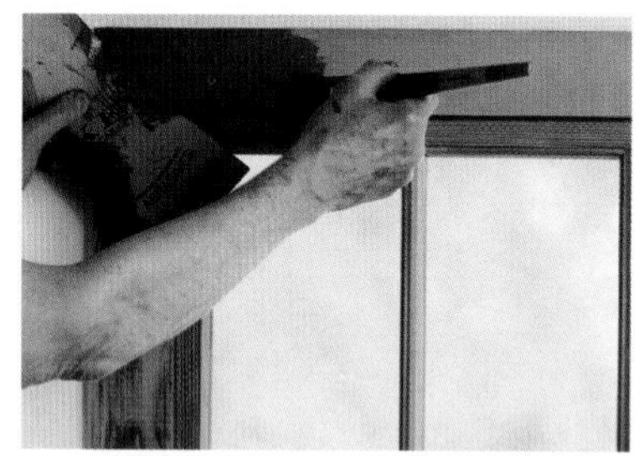

1 Sand the window frame with medium-grade sandpaper, then paint with pale blue-green vinyl silk paint and leave to dry. For the glaze, mix 1 part deep blue-green emulsion (latex) to 6 parts scumble. Paint the glaze over the main surfaces.

2 While the glaze is wet, draw the heart grainer (rocker) across the glazed surface, rocking it backwards and forwards. Wipe the corners with a damp cloth to make a mitre. As you work, protect the wet graining with a piece of sandpaper. Leave to dry.

3 Apply a coat of varnish only over the glazed areas and leave to dry. Paint the inner edges of the frame and the glazing bars across the window with glaze. While still wet, draw down each piece of wood with the rubber comb. Leave to dry, then apply another coat of varnish over the whole window frame.

4 Make sure that the glass is clean, and then attach the stencil with masking tape. Using a stencil brush, apply the frosting evenly through the stencil. Remove the stencil before the varnish dries completely.

CRACKLE-GLAZE PICTURE FRAME

This simple picture frame – which could also be used to hold a small mirror – is made from a piece of plywood. Simply cut a square from the centre and edge with beading. As well as being treated with crackle glaze, the brightly coloured paintwork is distressed slightly with sandpaper to give a very attractive finish.

YOU WILL NEED

- yellow ochre, turquoise, orange, lime green and bright pink emulsion (latex) paint
- medium and small decorator's brushes
- acrylic crackle glaze
- masking tape
- craft knife
- flat artist's paintbrush
- coarse-grade sandpaper
- acrylic varnish and brush

1 Paint the frame with two coats of yellow ochre emulsion (latex), allowing each to dry. Brush on a coat of crackle glaze. Leave to dry according to the manufacturer's instructions.

2 Place strips of masking tape in a pattern on either side of the frame, as shown.

3 Where the ends of the tape overlap, carefully trim off the excess with a craft knife.

4 Brush turquoise paint on the unmasked sections of the frame, working in one direction. The crackle effect will appear almost immediately. Take care not to overbrush an area (see Basic Techniques).

5 Brush orange paint on alternate sections of the pattern in the same way. Paint the remaining sections lime green.

6 Leave the paint to dry, and then carefully peel away the masking tape.

7 Using a flat artist's paintbrush, apply bright pink paint to the areas where the masking tape had been. Do this freehand to give the frame a handpainted look. Leave to dry.

8 Rub coarse-grade sandpaper over the crackled paint surface to reveal some of the yellow ochre paint beneath.

9 Seal the frame with two coats of acrylic varnish. Apply the first coat quickly, taking care not to overbrush and reactivate the crackle glaze.

SPONGED LAMP BASE

Three shades of green paint are sponged on to this inexpensive lamp base to give a very attractive dappled surface. If you prefer, you can practise the sponging technique first on a piece of white paper until you are confident. You will quickly discover that it is not at all difficult, despite the very professional-looking result.

YOU WILL NEED
- wooden lamp base with flex (electric cord) and light socket
- masking tape
- scissors
- rubber gloves
- fine wire (steel) wool
- acrylic primer
- flat artist's paintbrush
- off-white, jade green and emerald green emulsion (latex) paint
- bowl
- natural sponge
- white paper
- clear acrylic varnish and brush

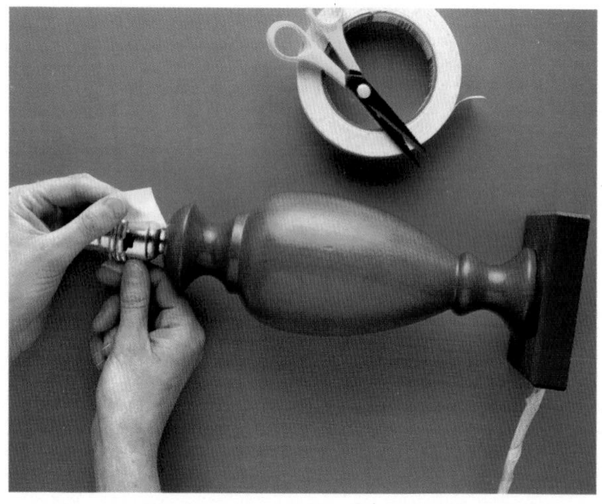

1 Cover the flex (electric cord) and light socket with layers of masking tape to protect them.

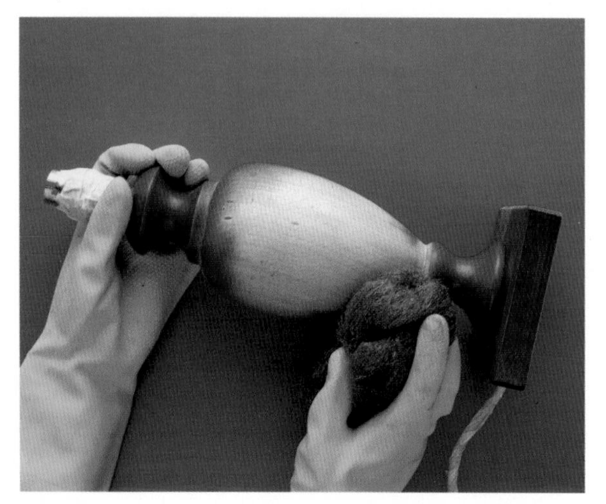

2 Wearing rubber gloves, rub down the existing varnish or paint with wire (steel) wool.

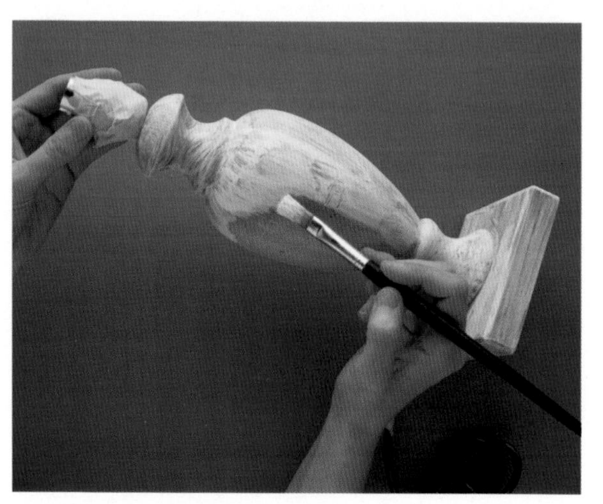

3 Paint the lamp base with two coats of acrylic primer, leaving each to dry.

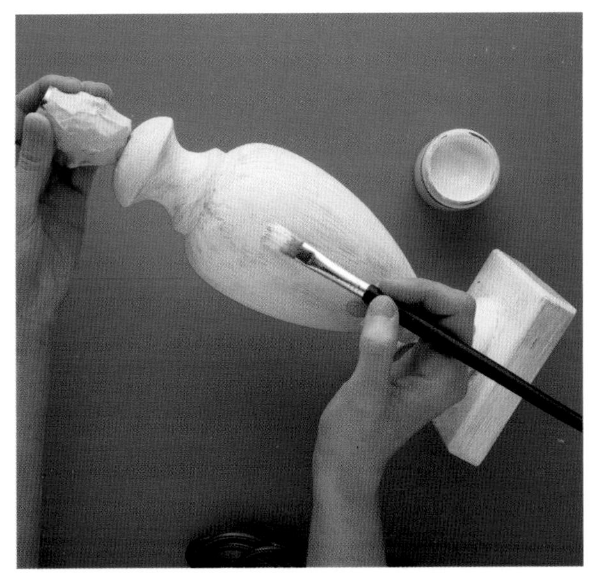

4 Paint with two coats of off-white emulsion (latex), leaving the paint to dry between coats.

5 Mix a 50/50 solution of jade green paint and water. Dampen the sponge and squeeze it until nearly dry, then dip it into the paint. Practise by dabbing the sponge on to a piece of white paper.

6 Cover the lamp base with a dappled layer of paint, applying it just a little at a time in order to build up the texture gradually.

7 Add some off-white paint to lighten the colour. Sponge this lightly over the first layer of colour. Break off a small piece of sponge and use this to work the colour into the moulding.

8 Mix a little emerald green paint 50/50 with water. Apply this mixture sparingly over the surface of the lamp base to add extra depth and texture. When dry, seal with three coats of varnish, allowing the varnish to dry thoroughly between coats. Finally, remove the protective masking tape from the flex and bulb fitting.

CRACKLE-GLAZE PLANTER

Here, crackle glaze is sandwiched between dark and pale layers of emulsion (latex) paint to give a modern planter an authentic antique look. The handpainted line is easier to do than you might think, and gives a smart finishing touch.

YOU WILL NEED
MDF planter
fine-grade sandpaper (optional)
emulsion (latex) paint in mid-blue and dark cream
small decorator's paintbrush
acrylic crackle glaze
fine artist's paintbrush
clear acrylic varnish and brush

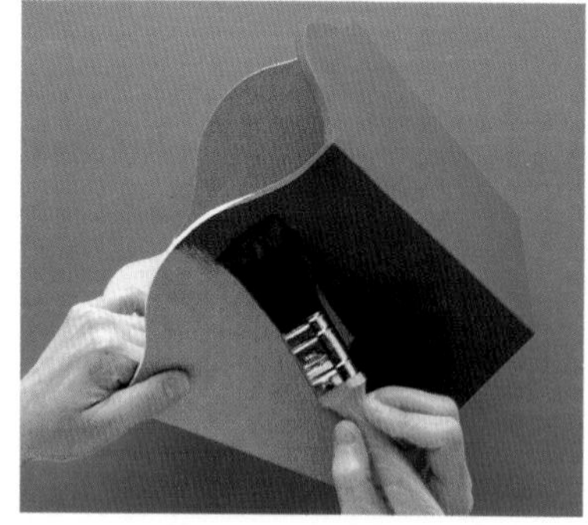

1 You do not need to prime MDF, but it may need sanding, especially on the cut edges. Paint the inside and outside with mid-blue emulsion (latex).

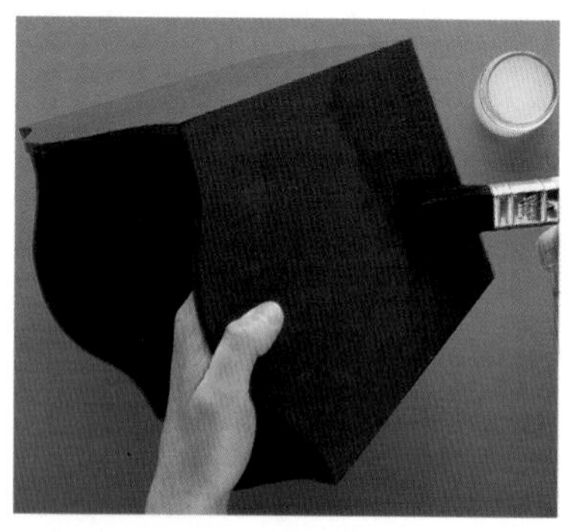

2 When the paint is completely dry, apply a layer of crackle glaze to the outside of the planter. Leave to dry.

3 Paint the outside of the planter with dark cream emulsion (latex). The crackled effect will start to appear almost immediately, so work as quickly as you can, with regular brushstrokes.

4 Holding your finger against the edge for support, paint a thin mid-blue line 1.5 cm/⅝ in from the edge on each side of the planter. Leave to dry, then seal with two coats of varnish.

SCANDINAVIAN TABLE

This pretty little table has been distressed by rubbing back thin layers of colour with fine wire wool. Focusing on the areas that would normally suffer most from general wear and tear gives an authentic aged look. The simple leaf design is painted freehand and picked out with paler highlights. If you are decorating a new wooden table, sand the wood first with fine-grade sandpaper and paint with a coat of primer. Remove the drawer knob.

YOU WILL NEED
MDF or wooden table with drawer
rubber gloves
fine wire (steel) wool
dark yellow, grey-green, white, mid-green and pale green emulsion (latex) paint
flat artist's paintbrush
small decorator's paintbrushes
acrylic scumble
fine artist's paintbrush
clear matt (flat) acrylic varnish and brush

1 Rub down the table with fine wire (steel) wool, wearing a pair of rubber gloves. Pay particular attention to the bevelled edges.

2 Using dark yellow emulsion (latex), paint the mouldings (if any) around the edge of the drawer and the tabletop.

3 Paint the rest of the table and the drawer front with two coats of grey-green emulsion (latex), allowing the paint to dry between coats.

4 Wearing rubber gloves once again, rub down the entire surface with wire wool.

5 Mix 50/50 white emulsion (latex) and scumble. Apply sparsely to the green areas with a dry brush, using light diagonal strokes and varying the angle of the brush to give an even coverage.

6 Mix 50/50 dark yellow emulsion (latex) and scumble. Paint this over the mouldings.

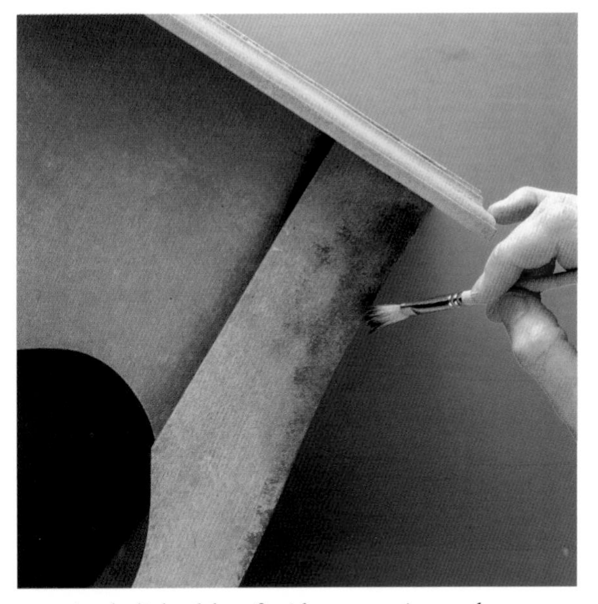

7 Apply light dabs of mid-green paint to the parts of the table that would receive the most wear: the top corners of the legs and underneath. Leave to dry, then rub back with wire wool.

8 Paint a scrolling leaf design around the edge of the drawer front in pale green. Pick out the stalks and leaf veins with fine brushstrokes in mid-green.

9 Still using the fine artist's paintbrush, add white and yellow highlights to the leaf design.

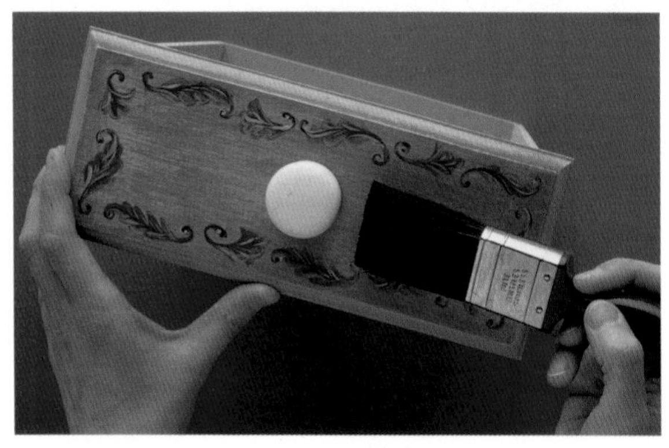

10 Seal the drawer and table with a coat of acrylic varnish for protection.

MATERIALS

Acrylic or emulsion (latex) paint and acrylic scumble glaze are the main materials you need to put a wide variety of paint techniques into practice.

ACRYLIC PRIMER is a quick-drying, water-based primer. It can be used to prime new wood.

ACRYLIC SCUMBLE is a slow-drying, water-based medium with a milky, gel-like appearance, which dries clear. It adds texture and translucency to the paint, and the marks you make with brushes, sponges and other tools are held in the glaze.

ACRYLIC VARNISH is available in a satin or matt (flat) finish. It is used to seal paint effects to give a more durable surface. Acrylic floor varnish is hardwearing and should be used on floors.

ARTIST'S ACRYLIC PAINT can be found in art and craft shops. It gives various paint effects a subtle translucent quality.

CRACKLE GLAZE is brushed on to a surface, causing the paint laid over it to crack in random patterns to create an aged appearance.

EMULSION (LATEX) PAINT is opaque and comes in a choice of matt (flat) or satin finish. Satin finish is usually best for the base colour and matt (flat) for paint effects. Use sample pots of paint if you need only a small amount.

METHYLATED SPIRIT (denatured alcohol) is a solvent that will dissolve emulsion (latex) paint and can be used to distress paint. It is also a solvent, thinner and brush cleaner for shellac.

PURE POWDER PIGMENT can be mixed with acrylic scumble, clear wax or emulsion (latex) paint. It is also used for vinegar graining.

SHELLAC is a type of varnish, available in clear and brown shades. French polish and button polish are in fact shellac and may be easier to find. It can be used to seal wood, metal leaf and paint.

WAX is available in neutral and in brown. It will seal and colour paint. Neutral wax can be mixed with powder pigment.

Opposite: 1 powder pigments, 2 emulsion (latex) paints, 3 acrylic primer, 4 artist's acrylic colours, 5 acrylic scumble, 6 crackle glaze, 7 neutral wax, 8 brown wax, 9 methylated spirit (denatured alcohol), 10 brown shellac, 11 clear shellac.

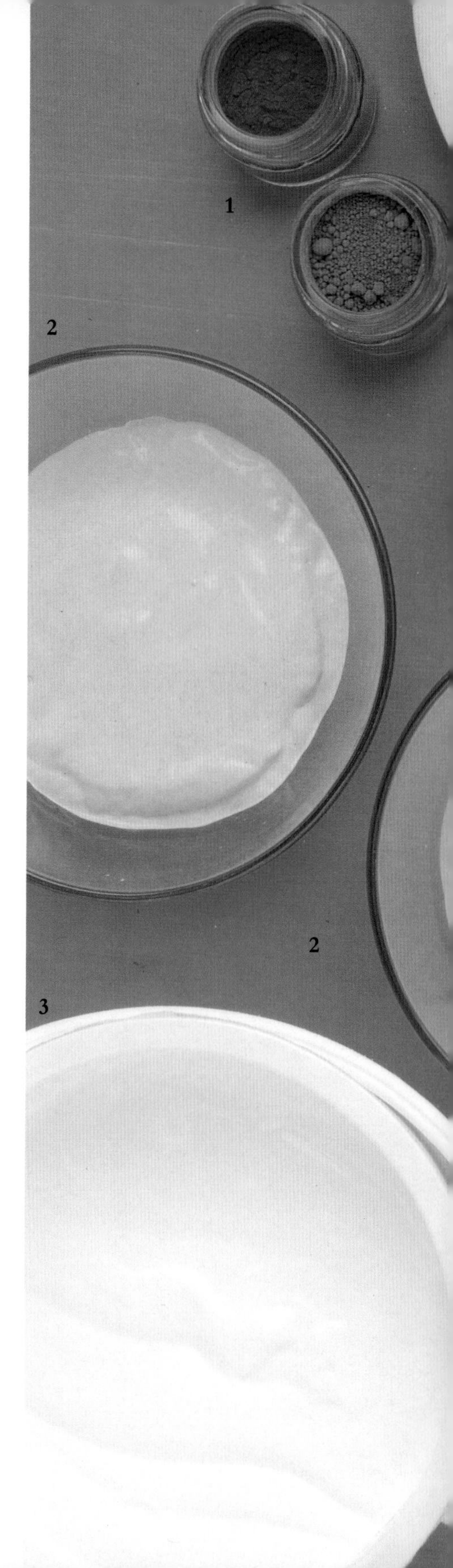

4
2
11
9
2
1
2
10
5
6
2
7
8

EQUIPMENT

Different paint effects require different tools. Most tools are cheap and easily found in DIY (hardware) or decorating suppliers.

ABRASIVES Sandpaper and wire (steel) wool come in many grades. They are used for distressing paint.

ARTIST'S PAINTBRUSHES are needed to paint fine detail.

DECORATOR'S PAINTBRUSHES are used to apply emulsion (latex) paint, washes and glazes. They come in a wide range of sizes.

FLAT VARNISH BRUSHES can be used for painting and varnishing. They are often the favourite choice of paint effect experts.

MASKING TAPE comes in many types. Easy-mask and low-tack tapes are less likely to pull off paintwork, and flexible tape is good for going around curves. Fine line tape is useful for creating a narrow negative line.

MEASURING EQUIPMENT A ruler, spirit (carpenter's) level, set square (T square) and plumb-line are needed to mark out designs.

MUTTON CLOTH (STOCKINET) is very absorbent and can be used for paint effects. Cotton cloths are also used for ragging and polishing.

NATURAL SPONGES are used for sponging. They are valued for their textural quality. Synthetic sponges can be used for colourwashing.

PAINT KETTLES, trays and pots are used to mix and store paint.

PAINT ROLLERS, small and large, are used for textured effects and to provide an even-textured base colour without brushmarks.

RUBBER COMBS AND HEART GRAINERS (ROCKERS) are used to create textured patterns in paint glazes. Heart grainers (rockers) create an effect of the heart grain of wood.

STENCIL BRUSHES are for stippling paint on to smaller surfaces.

STIPPLING BRUSHES, usually rectangular, are used to even out the texture of glaze and to avoid brushmarks.

Opposite: 1 paint containers, 2 spirit (carpenter's) level, 3 plumbline, 4 kitchen paper (paper towels), 5 artist's brushes, 6 decorator's brushes, 7 flat varnish brushes, 8 hog softening brush, 9 stencil brush, 10 paint rollers, 11 gloves, 12 stippling brush, 13 masking tapes, 14 measuring equipment, 15 craft knife and pencil, 16 heart grainer (rocker), 17 combs, 18 sponges, 19 mutton cloth (stockinet), 20 rag, 21 wire (steel) wool and sandpaper.

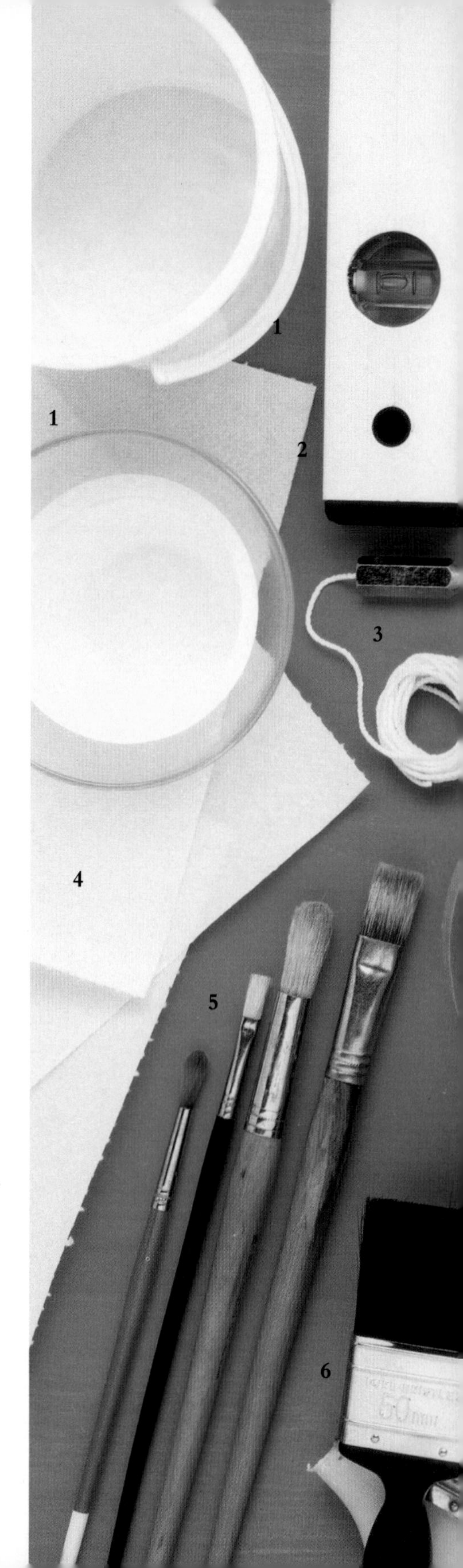

16
19
20
15
18
14
17
21
12
13
8
7
10
11
9

BASIC TECHNIQUES

Most of the projects in this book are based on a few simple techniques. These can be used on their own, or combined to produce an infinite variety of paint effects.

The techniques shown here all use ultramarine blue emulsion (latex) paint. This has been mixed with acrylic scumble glaze and/or water, as appropriate, to achieve the desired effect. Two coats of silk finish white emulsion (latex) paint were rollered on as a base. This provides an even-textured, non-absorbent finish, which is ideal to work on as it allows glazes to dry more slowly and evenly than emulsion (latex) paint and mistakes are easily wiped off.

All these techniques, except the crackle glaze, can be done with artist's acrylic paint mixed with scumble; then the effects will look more translucent.

Sponging

Dilute a little paint with a little water in a paint tray or saucer. Dip a damp, natural sponge into the paint and wipe off the excess on kitchen paper (paper towels). Dab the sponge on to the surface in different directions.

Sponging and dispersing

Follow the technique as for sponging, then rinse the sponge in clean water and dab it over the sponged paint before it dries to soften the effect.

Combing

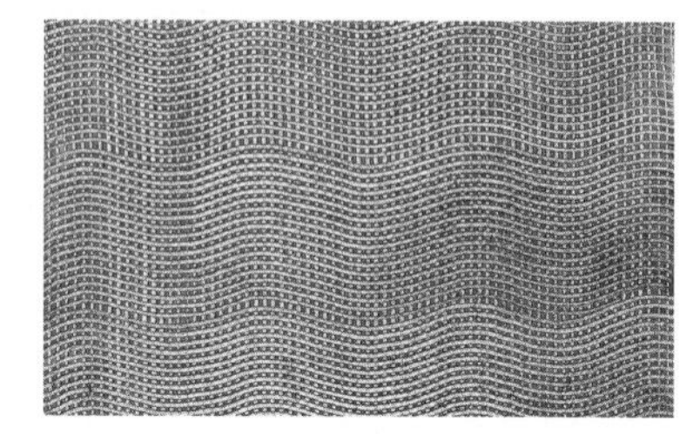

Mix paint with acrylic scumble and brush on with cross-hatched brushstrokes. Run a metal or rubber graining comb through the wet glaze. This pattern was done with straight vertical strokes and wavy horizontal ones.

Colourwashing

Dilute the paint with water and brush on randomly with cross-hatched brushstrokes, using a large decorator's brush. A damp sponge will give a similar effect.

Rubbing in colourwash

Dilute the paint with water and brush on. Use a clean cotton rag to disperse the paint. Alternatively, apply it directly with the rag and rub in.

Frottage

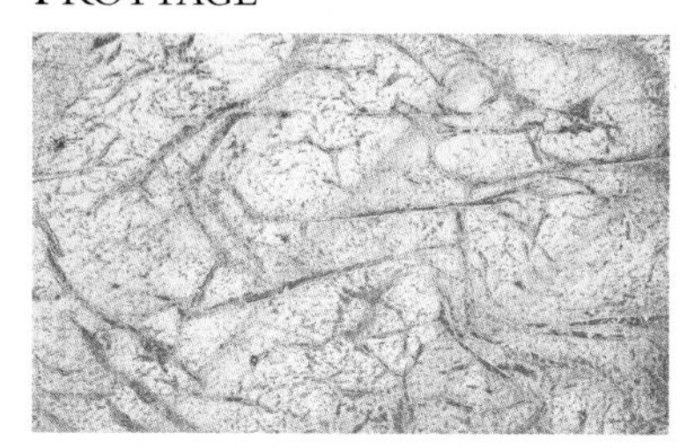

Apply paint with cross-hatched brushstrokes, then press a piece of tissue paper over the wet surface and peel it off. The paint can be diluted with water or scumble.

Dabbing with a mutton cloth (stockinet)

Brush on paint mixed with scumble, using cross-hatched brushstrokes. Dab a mutton cloth (stockinet) over the wet glaze to even out the texture and eliminate the brushstrokes.

Ragging

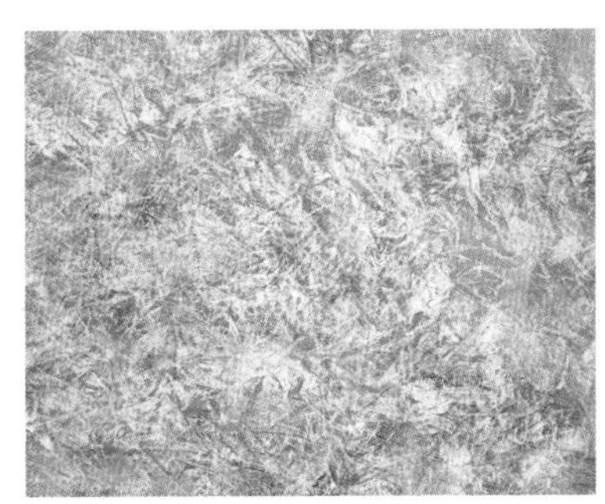

Mix paint with scumble and brush on, using cross-hatched brushstrokes. Scrunch up a piece of cotton rag and dab this in all directions, twisting your hand for a random look. When the rag becomes too paint-soaked, use a new one.

Rag rolling without brushmarks

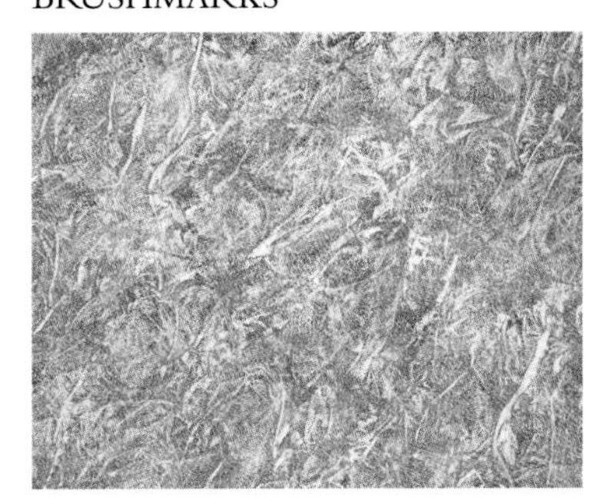

Brush on paint mixed with scumble and dab with a mutton cloth (stockinet) to eliminate brushmarks. Scrunch a cotton rag into a sausage shape and roll over the surface, changing direction as you go. Use a new piece of rag when it becomes too wet.

Stippling

Brush on paint mixed with acrylic scumble, using cross-hatched brushstrokes. Pounce a stippling brush over the wet glaze, working from the bottom upwards to eliminate brushmarks and provide an even-textured surface. Keep the brush as dry as possible by regularly wiping the bristles with kitchen paper (paper towels).

Dragging

Mix paint with scumble glaze and brush on with cross-hatched brushstrokes. Drag a flat decorator's brush through the wet glaze, keeping a steady hand. The soft effect shown here is achieved by going over the wet glaze again to break up the lines.

Crackle glaze

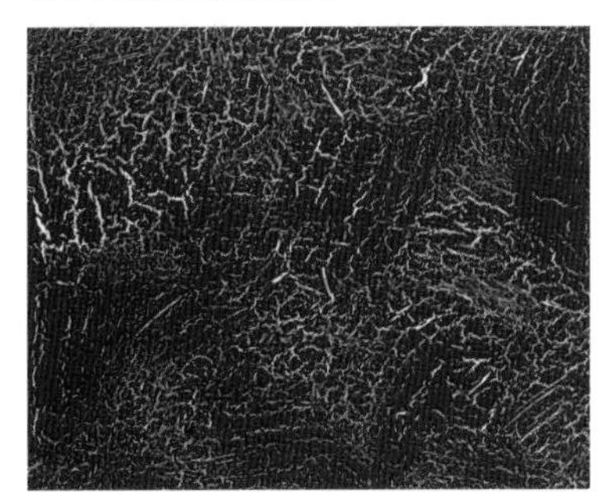

Brush on a coat of water-based crackle glaze and leave to dry according to the manufacturer's instructions. Using a well-laden brush, apply paint carefully on top so that you lay, rather than brush, it over the surface. Work quickly and do not overbrush an area already painted. If you have missed an area, touch it in when the paint has dried. Seal with acrylic varnish.

MIXING PAINTS AND GLAZES

There are no precise recipes for mixing glazes and washes. Generally speaking, the proportion of emulsion (latex) paint to scumble is 1 part paint to 6 parts scumble. This will give soft, semi-translucent colour that is suitable for effects such as ragging, dragging and combing where you want the coloured glaze to hold the marks you have made. If you want a more opaque coverage, you can reduce the amount of scumble, but as the paint will dry more quickly it may be harder to maintain a wet edge for an even result. When you are mixing scumble with artist's acrylic paint, the amount of paint you use depends on the depth of colour you need. Acrylic paint mixed with scumble gives a more translucent colour but it is used in exactly the same way as the emulsion (latex) mix.

If you do not need the texture provided by the scumble (for example, when colourwashing) but you want to dilute the colour, use water. This is cheaper but it dries more quickly, which may be a disadvantage. If you want to slow down the drying time, add a 50/50 mix of water and scumble to the paint. Emulsion (latex) paint can be diluted with any amount of water, and several thin washes of colour will give a more even cover than one thick wash.

Try to mix up enough colour to complete the area you are to decorate. It is difficult to gauge how much you will need. Washes and glazes stretch a long way, but if in doubt, mix up more than you think you might need. If you want to repeat the effect, measure the quantities you use. Before you start, painting samples on to part of the surface or scrap wood will give you the truest effect.

Ragging with acrylic paint and scumble.

Ragging with emulsion (latex) paint and scumble.

Colourwashing with one wash of equal parts emulsion (latex) paint and water.

Colourwashing with four thin washes of 1 part paint to 8 parts water to achieve the same colour saturation.

WORKING WITH COLOUR

Paint effects can vary widely according to your choice of colour and the way in which you use it. Whether you put a light colour over a dark base or a dark colour over a light one is a matter of choice, although a translucent pale colour would not really be visible over a dark base. A bright base colour can give added depth and a subtle glow beneath a dark top coat, while using the colours the other way round will tone down a bright colour. Tone-on-tone colour combinations are good for a subtle effect and are always a safe bet, but experiment with contrasting colours for exciting results.

Many of the techniques in this book use layers of several different colours. Greater depth and texture are achieved when you build up colours in this way, but a simple technique with one colour can be just as effective. It depends on the look you want and the furnishings in the room.

If you want to tone down a paint effect, you can lighten it by brushing over a wash of very diluted white or off-white emulsion (latex) paint. You can also tone down a colour by darkening it. A wash of raw umber paint works well over most colours and has a much warmer feel than black.

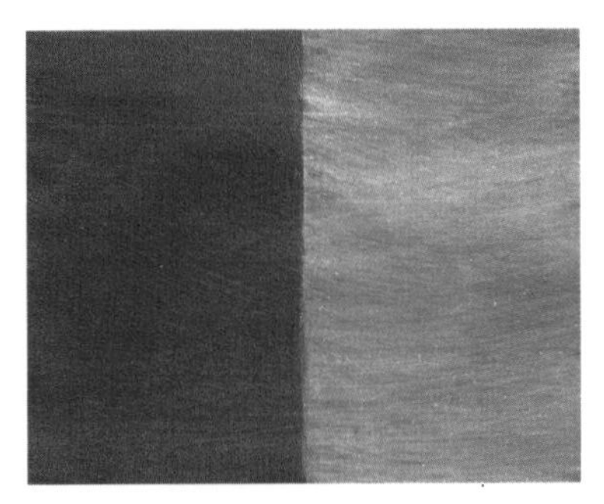

Adding white to lighten bright blue colourwashing.

Adding raw umber to darken bright red colourwashing.

Sponging – light yellow over deep yellow (*left*), deep yellow over light yellow (*right*).

Dabbing with a mutton cloth (stockinet) – dull green over emerald green (*left*), emerald green over dull green (*right*).

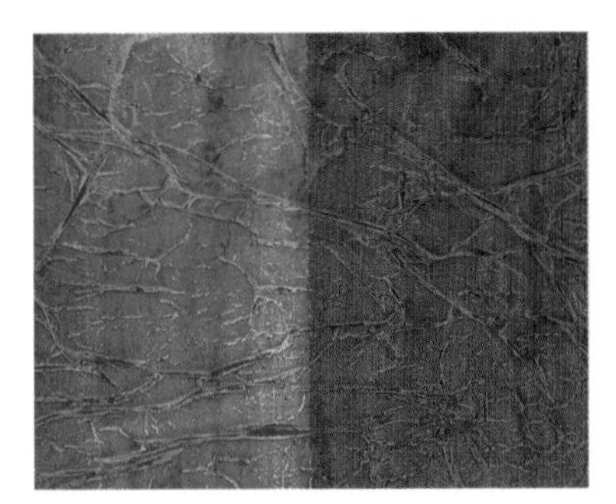

Frottage – tone-on-tone, deep blue over light blue (*left*), tone on contrast, bright blue over orange (*right*).

Colourwashing (*left*) in orange, red and crimson, finishing with the darkest colour.
Sponging (*right*) in three shades of blue-green, finishing with the lightest colour.

MIXING COLOURS

Emulsion (latex) paint is available in a huge range of ready-mixed colours. If you use acrylic paint or pure powder pigment you will need to mix your own colours.

Most colours can be mixed from yellow, cyan blue, magenta, black and white, but a basic palette of 14 colours plus black and white will allow you to mix an enormous range of colours. The suggested palette consists of yellow ochre, cadmium yellow, raw sienna, burnt sienna, red ochre, cadmium red, alizarin crimson, ultramarine blue, Prussian blue, cerulean blue, viridian green, oxide of chromium, raw umber and burnt umber. These basic colours are beautiful alone, and many other colours can be made by mixing them.

Some colour combinations are unexpected, and there are no hard-and-fast rules about which colours should or should not be mixed. If you experiment, you will soon develop confidence and a good eye for mixing colour.

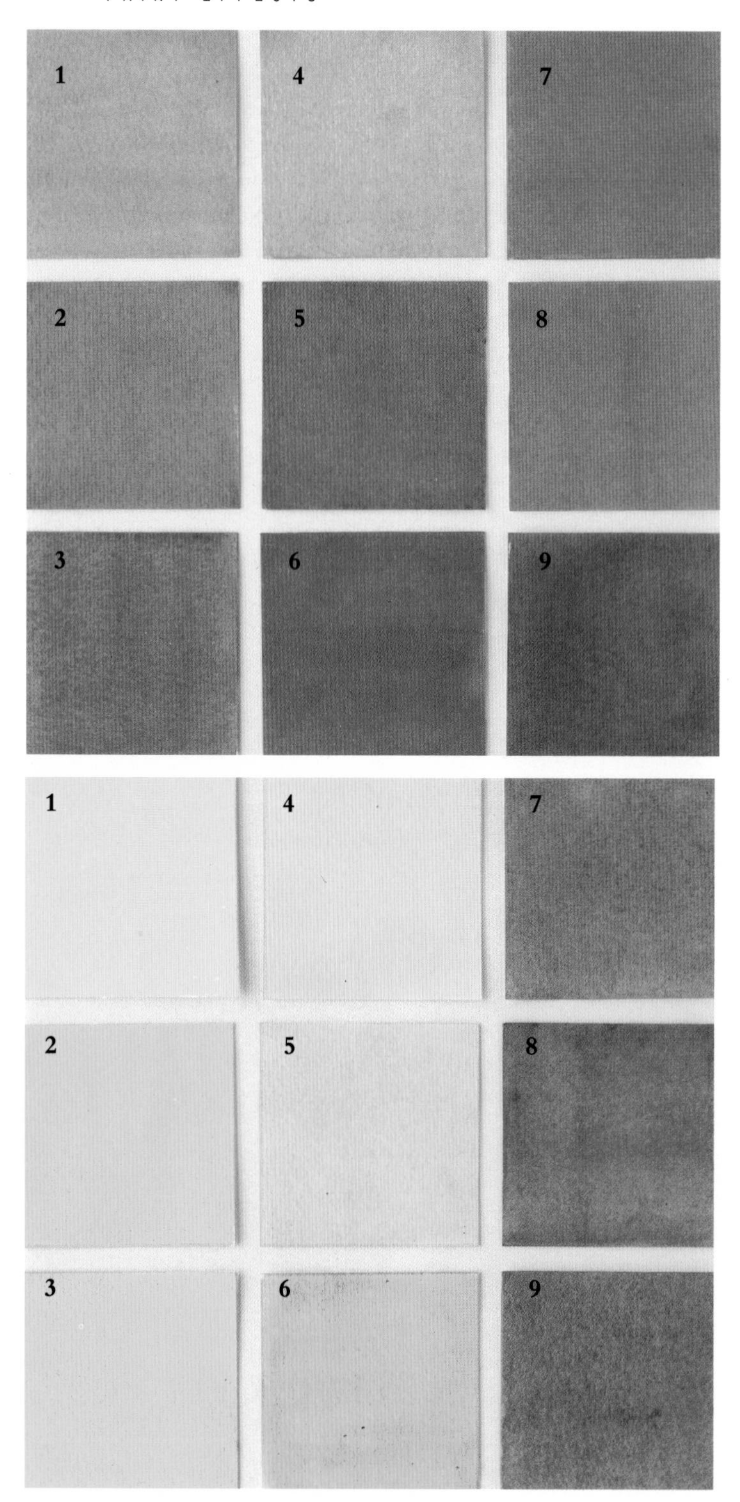

YELLOWS AND BROWNS (*right*)
1 Cadmium yellow and white
2 Cadmium yellow
3 Cadmium yellow and viridian green
4 Yellow ochre and white
5 Yellow ochre
6 Raw sienna
7 Burnt sienna
8 Burnt umber
9 Raw umber

REDS (*opposite*)
1 Alizarin crimson, cadmium yellow and white
2 Cadmium red and cadmium yellow
3 Red ochre
4 Red ochre and white
5 Cadmium red and burnt umber
6 Cadmium red
7 Cadmium red and black
8 Alizarin crimson
9 Alizarin crimson and oxide of chromium

BLUES (*top right*)
1 Cerulean blue, raw umber and white
2 Prussian blue, black and white
3 Prussian blue
4 Cerulean blue
5 Ultramarine blue and white
6 Ultramarine blue
7 Alizarin crimson, ultramarine blue and white
8 Alizarin crimson and ultramarine blue
9 Ultramarine blue and raw umber

GREENS (*right*)
1 Prussian blue, cadmium yellow and white
2 Prussian blue and cadmium yellow
3 Prussian blue and yellow ochre
4 Viridian green and cadmium yellow
5 Oxide of chromium
6 Ultramarine and yellow ochre
7 Prussian blue, yellow ochre and white
8 Viridian green, raw umber and white
9 Viridian green

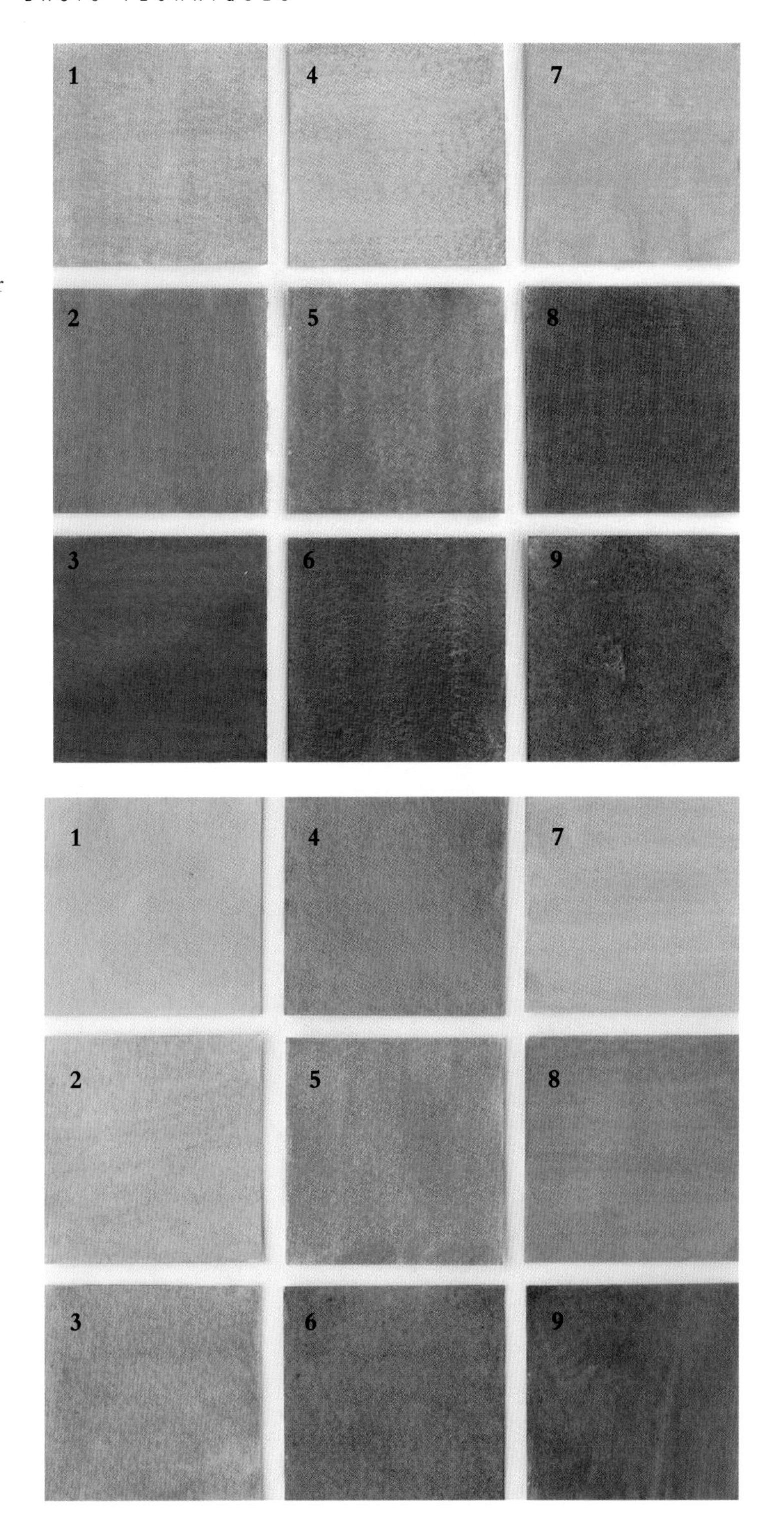

TEMPLATES

HARLEQUIN SCREEN

Diagrams to show how to mark the panels and apply the masking tape.

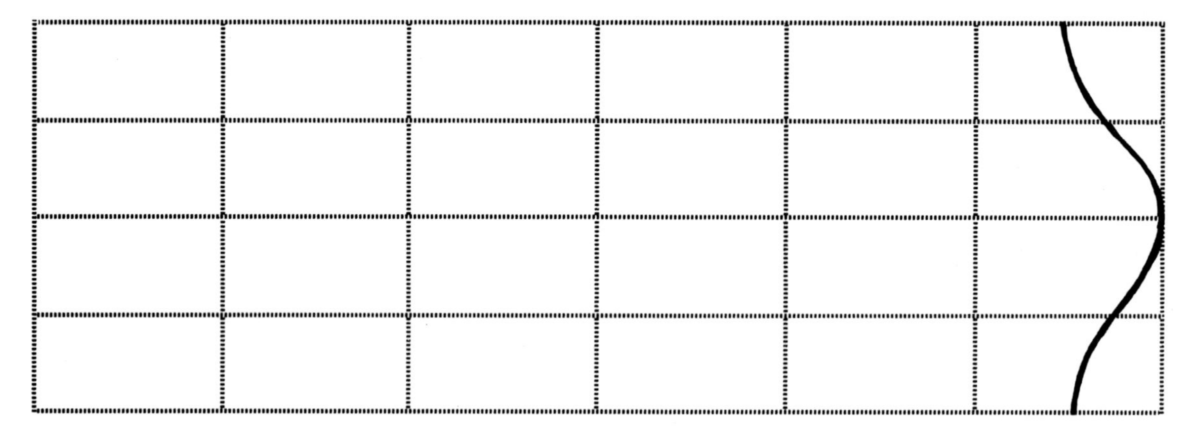

The pencil marks

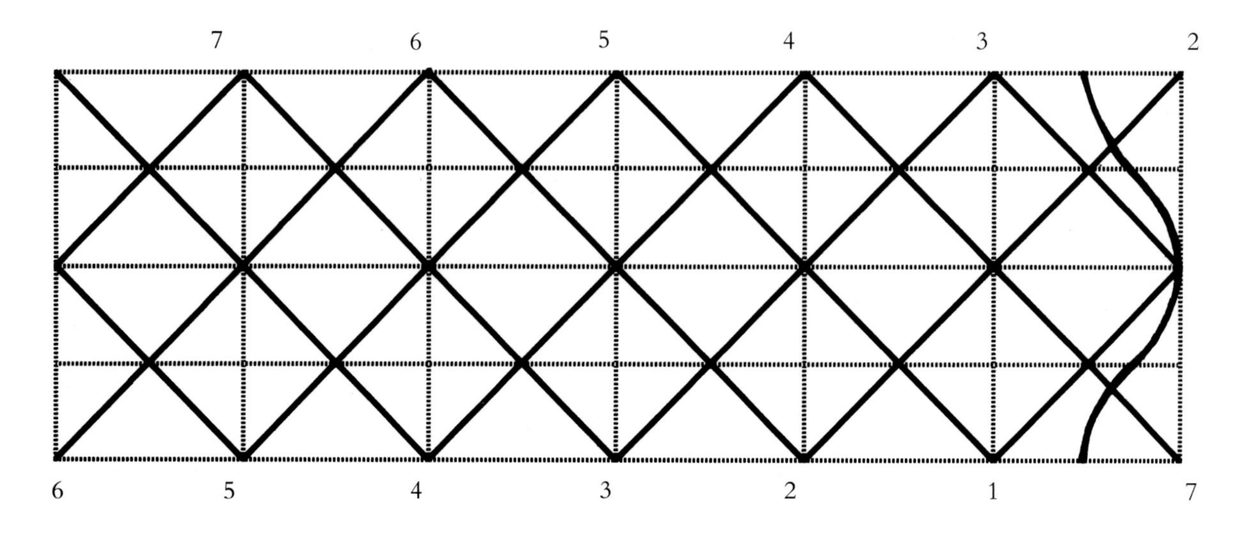

The tape marks

SUPPLIERS

Most materials required are available from decorating and art suppliers. The following list includes specialist suppliers.

Crown Paints
Crown House, Hollins Road,
Darwen, Lancs BB3 0BG, England

Dulux Australia
145 Cabarita Road, Concord,
NSW 23137, Australia

Dulux (Pty) Ltd
8 Juyn Street, PO Box 123704,
Alrode, South Africa

Foxell and James
57 Farringdon Road,
London EC1M 3JB, England

Green and Stone
259 Kings Road,
London SW3 5EL, England

W. Habberley Medows Ltd.
5 Saxon Way, Chelmsley Wood,
Birmingham B37 5AY, England

ICI
Hutt Park Road, PO Box 30749,
Lower Hutt, New Zealand

Paint Service Co. Ltd.
19 Eccleston Street,
London SW1W 9LX, England

Pascol Paints Australia Pty Ltd
PO Box 63, Rosebery,
NSW 2018, Australia

Paper and Paints
4 Park Walk,
London SW10 0AD, England

Wilson W. A. & Sons Inc
4 6 Industrial Park Drive,
Wheeling, WV 2603, USA

ACKNOWLEDGEMENTS

The publishers and author would like to thank the following people for contributing projects to this book:
Liz Wagstaff for the Diamond-stencilled Wall pp 10–12, Limewashed Wal pp 13–15, Fresco Effect pp 16–17, Blue-spotted Wall pp 28–9, Stone Wall 30–3, Wax-resist Shutters 34–6 and Hot Pink Wall pp 40–1; Sacha Cohen for the Two-tone Rollered Wall pp 25–7, Distressed Tabletop pp 56–8, Dry-Brushed Chair pp 59–61 and Grained Door pp 62–3; Judy Smith for the Trompe l'oeil Tuscan Wall pp 42–5; Elaine Green for the Vinegar-glazed Floorcloth pp 49–51, Harlequin Screen pp 64–7 and Grained Window Frame pp 68–9; Dinah Kelly for the Combed Check Floor pp 52–5 and Crackle-glaze Picture Frame pp 70–3 ; Lucinda Ganderton for the Sponged Lamp Base pp 74–7, Crackle-glaze Planter pp 78–9 and Scandinavian Table pp 80–3.

The publishers would also like to thank Nice Irmas, 46 Goodge Street, London W1P 1FJ (tel: 0171 580 6921) for loaning many items for photography.

INDEX